Opening up
Judges

SIMON J ROBINSON

DayOne

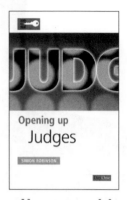

Opening up
Judges

SIMON ROBINSON

'A man slain by a tent peg. A superman dispatching his enemies with the jawbone of a donkey. Yet another man carving up a woman. It is all in the book of Judges, and it is all covered by Simon J Robinson in a way that makes these and other unusual events clear. This captivating presentation reads like a fast-paced story, but not content to be only a deft story-teller, the author constantly draws out spiritual principles that apply to life today. A very readable and gripping book!'

Roger Ellsworth,
Author, Pastor of Immanuel Baptist Church, Benton, Illinois, USA

'Someone once told me God is often at work in the messiest situations. Few periods of history are any messier than the dark days of the judges in Israel. Engaging with this book in the midst of a messy world will encourage you to see God is still in control.'

Dessie Maxwell,
Lecturer, Belfast Bible College, Northern Ireland

'Simon Robinson takes us on a whistle-stop tour of dark and heroic events from over 3,000 years ago, and ably applies their significance to a twenty-first-century world of economic progress and moral decay.'

Rev Dr Steve Brady
Principal, Moorlands College, Christchurch, England

© Day One Publications 2006
First printed 2006

All Scripture quotations, unless otherwise indicated, are taken from
the NIV, International Bible Society,
1973, 1978, 1984.

ISBN 978-1-84625-043-9

9 781846 250439 >

British Library Cataloguing in Publication Data available

Published by Day One Publications
Ryelands Road, Leominster, HR6 8NZ
Telephone 01568 613 740   FAX 01568 611 473

email—sales@dayone.co.uk
web site—www.dayone.co.uk
North American—e-mail-sales@dayonebookstore.com
North American web site—www.dayonebookstore.com

Designed by Steve Devane and printed by Gutenberg Press, Malta

Overview   8

❶ From victory to defeat (1:1-3:6)   10

❷ Expect the unexpected (3:7-31)   17

❸ God at work (4:1-5:31)   24

❹ The man who made a difference (6:1-32)   32

❺ Let the battle commence! (6:33-7:25)   40

❻ The enemy within (8:1-32)   47

❼ Life without God (8:33-9:57)   52

❽ Watch your words! (10:1-11:40)   59

❾ The war of words (12:1-15)   67

❿ A woman after God's heart (13:1-25)   72

⓫ A man full of flaws (14:1-15:20)   79

⓬ The fall of a fool (16:1-31)   90

⓭ Dangerous assumptions (17:1-13)   98

⓮ Violent developments (18:1-31)   103

⓯ What lies beneath (19:1-30)   108

⓰ Chain reaction (20:1-21:25)   114

Further reading   120

Endnotes   121

Dedicated to
Benjamin James Robinson, my first grandchild

Acknowledgement
My sincere appreciation to the Rev Clive Anderson for the
help he has given me in clarifying matters pertaining to the
historical and geographical background of the Judges

List of Bible abbreviations

THE OLD TESTAMENT		1 Chr.	1 Chronicles	Dan.	Daniel
		2 Chr.	2 Chronicles	Hosea	Hosea
Gen.	Genesis	Ezra	Ezra	Joel	Joel
Exod.	Exodus	Neh.	Nehemiah	Amos	Amos
Lev.	Leviticus	Esth.	Esther	Obad.	Obadiah
Num.	Numbers	Job	Job	Jonah	Jonah
Deut.	Deuteronomy	Ps.	Psalms	Micah	Micah
Josh.	Joshua	Prov.	Proverbs	Nahum	Nahum
Judg.	Judges	Eccles.	Ecclesiastes	Hab.	Habakkuk
Ruth	Ruth	S.of.S.	Song of Solomon	Zeph.	Zephaniah
1 Sam.	1 Samuel	Isa.	Isaiah	Hag.	Haggai
2 Sam.	2 Samuel	Jer.	Jeremiah	Zech.	Zechariah
1 Kings	1 Kings	Lam.	Lamentations	Mal.	Malachi
2 Kings	2 Kings	Ezek.	Ezekiel		

THE NEW TESTAMENT		Gal.	Galatians	Heb.	Hebrews
		Eph.	Ephesians	James	James
Matt.	Matthew	Phil.	Philippians	1 Peter	1 Peter
Mark	Mark	Col.	Colossians	2 Peter	2 Peter
Luke	Luke	1 Thes.	1 Thessalonians	1 John	1 John
John	John	2 Thes.	2 Thessalonians	2 John	2 John
Acts	Acts	1 Tim.	1 Timothy	3 John	3 John
Rom.	Romans	2 Tim.	2 Timothy	Jude	Jude
1 Cor.	1 Corinthians	Titus	Titus	Rev.	Revelation
2 Cor.	2 Corinthians	Philem.	Philemon		

Overview

Once the Promised Land had been conquered, the people of Israel should have entered into a time of consolidation that would have taken them from strength to strength. Instead they took their eyes off God and became attracted to the idols worshipped by the nations around them. This ushered them into the time of great turmoil which we read about in the book of Judges.

Disobedience to God's Word will always create problems for his people and in this case it involved them being given into their enemies' hands. But God was faithful to them and when they cried out to him for help he sent saviours—who were called judges—to rescue them from the oppression they were suffering. The New Testament speaks of them as people of faith (see Hebrews 11:32).

The book of Judges covers a turbulent time in the Middle East as nations vied for supremacy. The Israelites should have been an example to the people around them, but instead they adapted to their pagan mindset and worshipped their idols.

This action-packed book has a powerful message for today because the period of the judges in which 'everyone did what was right in his own eyes' (Judges 21:25, ESV) is being lived out again in the twenty-first century. Let us be inspired by the judges whom God raised up to lead his people to victory, and be warned against engaging in the compromise shown by God's people during this period.

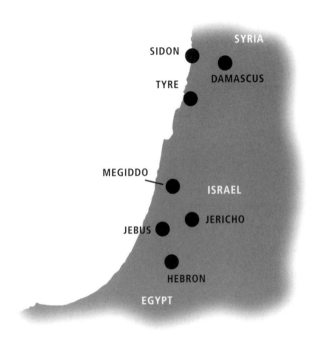

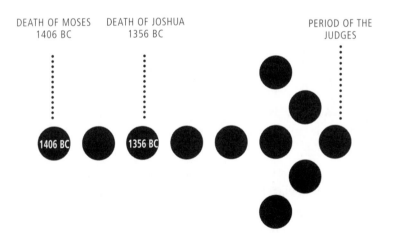

1 From victory to defeat

(1:1-3:6)

It had been forty years since Joshua triumphantly led the Israelites into the Promised Land. A new generation had emerged but there were still pockets of resistance from the Canaanites, Hittites and Philistines. It was time for God's people to complete the conquest!

The first flush of victory (1:1-19)

The people of Israel began by asking God to show them who should be 'the first to go up and fight ... against the Canaanites' (v. 1). He responded by assuring them that he would give the enemy into their hands and by instructing the tribe of Judah to lead the attack. They sprang into action—with the tribe of Simeon at their side—and fought in the hills (vv. 9-15), on the southern lowlands (vv. 16-17), and in the coastal regions (v. 18). And their strategy was successful because 'the LORD' was with them (v. 19).

The first sign of failure (1:19-21)

After such a positive start we would expect the success to continue, but in verse 19 we are told that 'they were unable to drive the people from the plains, because they had iron chariots'. These iron-clad chariots were notoriously difficult to engage in battle and would have given their enemy a distinct advantage. When Israel's ancestors were escaping Egypt, the enemy had lightweight chariots but the LORD gave them victory. Now they faced a new challenge, but the same God was fighting for them and they would have known victory if they had remembered that 'the LORD was with [them]' (v. 19).

Incomplete victories (1:22-36)

The focus now moves to the battle in the north of the country. Although ground was being gained they could not attain total victory. The writer tells us that they did not drive out their enemies and he repeats the phrase a further six times (in vv. 27-33) as if to highlight their failure. Eventually the northern tribes gained the edge and had the opportunity to drive out their enemies, but instead they chose to use them for forced labour (vv. 30,33,35).

A message (2:1-3)

The 'angel of the LORD' came to them. This manner of appearance is known as a theophany, a visible manifestation of God. His message was clear and challenging. Firstly, he spoke about the covenant that bound the people to him (v. 1b). He reminded them that he had brought their forefathers out of Egypt, forbidden them to establish a relationship with the people who lived in the land and required them to 'break down their altars' (vv. 1-2). Secondly, he exposed their failure to obey him (v. 2b). And thirdly, he announced his intention to leave these enemies in the land so that they would be 'thorns in [their] sides' (v. 3).

Crocodile tears (2:4-5)

The people wept and offered sacrifices to God to seek forgiveness for their sins and their faithlessness. On the surface this seems to be a positive response to God's word. But as we continue to read the book we will see that it was an empty gesture, because there was no change in their lives or their attitude towards God.

At the beginning of the book the new generation sought the Lord and were ready to face the challenge to consolidate Joshua's conquest of the Promised Land. But within the first two chapters we are disappointed with news of faithlessness, defeat and despair. Sadly this is a pattern that will be repeated many times.

Ever-decreasing circles

There was once a television programme in the UK called *Ever-decreasing circles*[1] and this is a very fitting description for the pattern of events that we discover in Judges.

The book is structured around a series of 'ever-decreasing circles': the people of Israel break the covenant—their binding agreement with the Lord—by lacking faith in the living God and worshipping idols. He punishes them by sending their enemies against them. After a period of suffering, they cry out to God for help and he sends a judge (an upholder and administrator of God's law) to deliver them. No sooner has the judge died than the people begin to worship idols and the same pattern of events occurs, each time worse than the one that preceded it.

Challenge and encouragement

This dynamic book forces us to look at our own lives and ask ourselves if we are compromising by worshipping the idols of our age. They may not be the kind of images that the Israelites bowed down to; the idols we worship are often material things that become more important to us than God or they may be personal advancement and pride. But, on the positive side, the faith and courage of the judges should encourage us to live for God in this age of faithlessness and compromise.

The generation game (2:6-23)

We have already been told about the people of Israel's failure to consolidate Joshua's earlier conquests (1:1-2:5). Now we are shown some of the spiritual problems which led to their defeat and drew them into the seven 'ever-decreasing circles'. We are shown this through the experiences of two generations.

The faithful generation (2:6-9)

The first generation fought with Joshua and conquered the Promised Land. After his death each tribe needed to settle into its allotted territory and root out the last elements of resistance (as described in 1:1-2:5). They had personally witnessed the 'the great things the LORD had done for Israel' and continued to serve the Lord throughout their lives (2:7).

The lost generation (2:10-23)

The new generation established a pattern of behaviour that repeats itself throughout the book. They 'knew neither the LORD, nor what he had done for Israel' (2:10). Consequently they deserted God by worshipping a Canaanite deity, Baal, along with other gods. This behaviour 'provoked the LORD to anger' (2:12), causing him to give them over to their enemies. When they were 'in distress' God raised up judges to save them (vv. 15-16). But after the judge died they returned to faithlessness, disobedience and idolatry.

> The new generation established a pattern of behaviour that repeats itself throughout the book. They 'knew neither the LORD, nor what he had done for Israel' (2:10). Consequently they deserted God by worshipping a Canaanite deity, Baal, along with other gods.

The test (3:1-6)

The writer now reflects on the generation who had failed to drive out the inhabitants of Canaan (see 1:1-2:5) from a different perspective. While they were responsible for the lack of faith which led to their defeat, God used their failure to test them (v. 1). In the original language the word translated 'test' means to prove something, or to show what something or someone is really made of. Sadly the way in which these people worshipped idols disclosed that their hearts were far from God.

The Lord had left some of the Israelites' enemies in the land in order to train them (v. 2). Life in Canaan was not going to be easy; battles would be fought and problems would persist. And God allowed them to face pressure from their enemies so that they would not grow feeble and complacent.

There are times when God leaves things unresolved in our lives. A job rejection we did not expect, a conflict with a Christian who refuses to be reconciled with us, a situation in our church that we are not entirely happy with or a heartache in the family. God will not always keep our lives neat and tidy; he will do things we do not expect and take us into situations we may find difficult so that we depend on him and grow in our faith. This was the apostle Paul's experience: on three occasions he asked the Lord to remove a 'thorn in [his] flesh' but the Lord spoke to him and said, 'My grace is sufficient for you, for my power is made perfect in weakness' (2 Cor. 12:9).

For further study ▶

FOR FURTHER STUDY

1. Joshua 24 provides us with an account of the way in which the Israelites renewed their covenant with the Lord shortly before Joshua's death. In verse 14 Joshua tells them to 'fear the LORD and serve him with all faithfulness' and to 'throw away [their] gods'. Compare the people's response in verses 16-17 and 24 with the charges brought against them in Judges 2:1-4. What were the main reasons behind their failure to follow through the pledge that had been made at Shechem?

2. How might the principles set out in 1 Peter 1:13-17 help us to carry through the commitment that we have made to the Lord?

3. Hebrews 11:32 lists some of the judges. What can we learn from them about living for God in an age of faithlessness and compromise?

TO THINK ABOUT AND DISCUSS

1. The people of Israel responded to the message from the angel by offering sacrifices but it was not accompanied by any change in their attitude and conduct. Look up James 1:22-24 and consider how you should make sure that your response to God's Word is genuine. Are there ways in which you can record and review the Bible passages through which God has challenged you?

2. How valid is repentance without real change in our attitude and conduct?

Think about specific sins you have confessed to God. What steps do you need to take, with God's help, to change in these areas?

2 Expect the unexpected

(3:7-31)

Before I went into the ministry I worked with someone who was very predictable. He would arrive at the office at 8:15 a.m., hang up his hat and coat, say 'Good morning', make a cup of tea, sit down and get on with his work. At noon he would heave a sigh, put his hat and coat on and go out to lunch. He returned at 12:55 and worked quietly for the rest of the afternoon. At 4:58 p.m. he washed his cup and he left the office at 5:00. And the next day he began the same routine again.

The pattern of events we read about in the chapters that follow seem as predictable as my former colleague: the people sinned, God gave them over to their enemies, they cried out to him in distress and he sent a judge to deliver them. Now we are shown some of the spiritual problems which led to their defeat and drew them into a series of 'ever-decreasing circles', but the only predictable element is the fickleness of God's people. God, however, moved in many wonderful and even shocking ways to bring them back to himself.

A model judge (vv. 7-10)

God had given the Israelites into the hands of Cushan-Rishathaim, the king of Mesopotamia. He was a ruthless man whose name meant 'Cushan of double wickedness' and it is likely that the name was given to him by those who had suffered violence at his hands.[2]

After the Israelites had cried out to the Lord he 'raised up' a judge, called Othniel, and he was just the kind of man you would expect to be a judge. Othniel was Caleb's nephew and had won the hand of his daughter in marriage through his bravery (Josh. 15:17). By this time he would have been an elder statesman (probably around seventy-five years of age) commanding the respect of the population.

Although Othniel was very well qualified he did not defeat Cushan-Rishathaim through his own efforts: 'The Spirit of the LORD came upon him, so that he became Israel's judge and went to war. The LORD gave Cushan-Rishathaim king of Aram into the hands of Othniel, who overpowered him' (v. 10).

A new enemy (vv. 12-14)

A new generation surfaced and, having forsaken God, they had been given over into the hands of Eglon, the king of Moab. He had allied himself with two of Israel's old enemies—the Ammonites and Amalekites—and their armies swept into the territory belonging to the tribes living beyond the Jordan. King Eglon made the 'City of Palms' his capital and reduced the Israelites to servitude for eighteen years. The city was also known as 'Jericho'; it was the first great success in the conquest of Caanan and a symbol of God's blessing on Joshua and the twelve tribes. Now it had become an emblem of defeat.

An unlikely judge (vv. 15-16)

The next man God raised up seems an unlikely candidate for a judge. He was Ehud, who is described as 'a left-handed man'; literally he was 'hindered in his right hand', which implies that he suffered from a deformed hand. It is not just Ehud's physical disabilities that mark him out as different from his predecessor: there is no mention of the power of God's Spirit, which came upon Othniel, nor of an immediate call from God to fight the enemy to his name.

Initially Ehud appears to be more of a Neville Chamberlain than a Winston Churchill, pursuing peaceful negotiation rather than aggressive action. He had been chosen to take the annual tribute to the king of Moab. This was the equivalent of 'protection money'; if they paid the Moabites a sum of money they would be left alone. The process of making the payment was designed to humiliate them. Every year a leading member of the community had to travel to Moab's capital and personally present the money to the king. On this occasion it was to be Ehud, but he was on a covert mission; only he and God knew that a weapon was hidden under his clothing (v. 16).

A pointed message (vv. 17-22)

The writer describes a scene of high drama. King Eglon made a majestic entry, clothed in his royal splendour and flanked by his courtiers. Ehud came in, probably demonstrating the kind of subservience the king expected of him. Gifts would have been presented, submission would have been expressed and the humiliating ritual was brought to a close. It was time for Ehud to leave the king's presence. But he split off from the larger group and went to the room where the king had received him to tell him that he had 'a secret message' (v. 19). The king's curiosity was aroused, so he sent out his servants and got out of his seat in anticipation; but the message was more pointed than he expected! The writer describes it graphically: 'Ehud reached with his left hand, drew the sword from his right thigh and plunged it into the king's belly. Even the handle sank in after the blade, which came out of his back. Ehud did not pull the sword out, and the fat closed in over it' (vv. 21-22).

> Crucifixion was one of the most brutal forms of execution that had been invented; it was an insult to Jews and an object of cursing from God (Gal. 3:10). Yet it was the means of our salvation; and the message of the cross has shocked people for generations.

These verses may not be our choice for a nice little devotion, but we have to remember that they describe desperate measures for dark times. God can work in the most unexpected ways. Just think about the cross—you could not have a crueller scene than that of an innocent man being put to death at the demand of a vengeful mob. Crucifixion was one of the most brutal forms of execution that had been invented; it was an insult to Jews and an object of cursing from God (Gal. 3:10). Yet it was the means of our salvation; and the message of the cross has shocked people for generations. Paul tells us that 'Jews demand miraculous signs and Greeks look for wisdom, but we preach Christ crucified: a stumbling block to Jews and foolishness to Gentiles' (1 Cor. 1:22-23).

Escape to victory (vv. 23-30)

After the king had been killed, Ehud made a swift, advantageous escape, locking Eglon's body in the room. The servants assumed that their master was relieving himself and waited 'to the point of embarrassment', when they finally opened the door and found him dead. By that time Ehud had put a significant distance between the palace and himself.

As soon as he arrived in home territory he called the people to follow him and attack the Moabites because 'the LORD has given Moab, your enemy, into your hands' (v. 28). As a result 10,000 Moabites were killed and the Israelites were delivered from oppression.

The victory brought about a striking role reversal: 'Moab was made subject to Israel, and the land had peace for eighty years' (v. 30). On the day that Ehud travelled to Jericho to symbolize his people's subservience to the king of Moab, God turned things upside down! Now the Moabites were the ones under subjection.

This should give us hope for the difficult times we face. God has a way of changing our circumstances at the most unexpected times and in the most unlikely ways. And remember: our final victory is assured! That is why the apostle Paul—after describing a time in which he was 'under great pressure, far beyond [his] ability to endure'—was able to say 'thanks be to God, who always leads us in triumphal procession' (2 Cor. 1:8; 2:14).

A mystery man (v. 31)

After Ehud's covert mission we are given a brief description of Shamgar and we find that another mould is broken. He was neither a man of impeccable pedigree (like Othniel) nor of visible deformity (like Ehud). But he struck down 600 Philistines—in what Alfred Edersheim described as an act of 'sudden sacred enthusiasm'[3]—and fought the enemy before they gained a foothold. Shamgar represented a sudden shift in the way in which the Lord was at work, reminding us that with God we must expect the unexpected!

FOR FURTHER STUDY

1. Compare Othniel's bravery (Josh. 15:13-17) with the confidence expressed by Caleb when he brought Moses a report about the Promised Land (Num. 13:25-33). What are the qualities that Othniel shared with his father-in-law? How would this have equipped him to be a judge?

2. In Judges 3 we find that, after Othniel, God used an unlikely man to bring deliverance to the Israelites. How do the following verses help us to appreciate the way in which God uses all kinds of people and circumstances to bring about his will: Psalm 22:26; 66:7; Proverbs 16:33; Genesis 50:20; Acts 17:26?

TO THINK ABOUT AND DISCUSS

1. Look up Proverbs 16:3,9,33 and Romans 8:28. What kind of attitude should we have towards the surprises and disappointments we face? Think about this in relation to people who mean you harm, or circumstances which do not seem to make any sense to you.

2. Although Othniel fitted the mould we may have expected for a judge, Ehud and Shamgar were different. What does this tell us about the uniqueness of each of God's servants? How much should you model yourself on another person (other than Jesus)?

3 God at work

(4:1-5:31)

Another 'ever-decreasing circle' had begun. Ehud was dead, the Israelites had forsaken the Lord and he had given them into the hands of their enemies.

The Canaanites are coming! (4:1-3)

The previous conflict centred on the south of the country (the City of Palms, which was Jericho) but in this instance the action took place in the north. The new oppression came by the hand of Jabin—a Canaanite king—and his ruthless general, Sisera. We have already seen that the Canaanites should have been driven out of the Promised Land but that instead the tribe of Naphtali used them as forced labour (1:33,35; cf. Josh. 1:10). The book of Joshua tells us that their capital, Hazor, had been burned down and destroyed (Josh. 11:10-11). But it appears that during the time the Israelites were oppressed by Moab, the Canaanites were able to regroup and rebuild their capital, nine miles north of Galilee. They had become a formidable enemy and the events that we read about in this chapter took place when military hardware became more sophisticated.

Deborah describes the tyranny inflicted by the Canaanites in her song. They had a stranglehold on the economy by blocking the major trade routes (5:6). They attacked the Israelites when they were defenceless (5:8) and captured and raped their women (5:30). This continued for twenty years until the Israelites came to their senses and cried out to the Lord for help.

A mother in Israel (4:4-5)

In response to their plea, the Lord raised up a prophetess called Deborah. She was one of the most remarkable people to emerge during the 350 year period charted in this book. Deborah was the first prophet since Moses' day and one of only three women prophets we read about in the Old Testament, the others being Miriam (Exod. 15:20) and Huldah (1 Kings 22:14).

Deborah was based in the south of the nation but the action took place in the north. She described herself as 'a mother in Israel' (5:7) and 'held court' under a tree that became known as 'the Palm of Deborah' (4:5). The Hebrew word translated 'held court' was used to describe the way in which a magistrate would settle disputes. This was very important at a time when the infrastructure of the nation had broken down and the normal channels for justice did not exist.

There could not be a greater contrast between the oppressor and the deliverer: a monster who held the tribes of

Israel in his iron grip and a mother who led them with a gentle hand. We may feel helpless in the face of our spiritual and moral enemies but we must never forget that God 'chose the weak things of the world to shame the strong' (1 Cor. 1:27). As an old saying goes: 'one plus God is a majority'!

Time for action (4:6-16)

Deborah sent for a man called Barak. He was probably a military leader and he came from Kedesh, a region which was particularly affected by Jabin's aggression. Barak travelled a dangerous seventy-mile journey to reach Deborah and when they met she told him that the Lord had commanded him to lead his people into battle. God had given Deborah an ingenious plan which she recounted to Barak: he was to gather 10,000 men and take them to the top of Mount Tabor. This would have given them a spectacular view of the Kishon valley, where God was going to draw out Sisera's troops.

Although the upper part of the valley would have been dry in the summer, the early spring rains swelled the river and made the whole valley waterlogged. This conflict took place during the dry season but God brought about unseasonable rains that swelled the river, filled the valley with water and brought the iron chariots to a standstill.

Although the details in 4:12-15 are concise, Deborah's song of celebration gives us a glimpse of the way in which God was at work:

> O LORD, when you went out from Seir,
> when you marched from the land of Edom,
> the earth shook, the heavens poured,
> the clouds poured down water...

From the heavens the stars fought,

from their courses they fought against Sisera.

The river Kishon swept them away,

the age-old river, the river Kishon.

March on, my soul; be strong!

(5:4, 20-21).

Barak and his men were facing a formidable enemy who possessed state of the art military hardware while 'not a shield or spear was seen among forty thousand in Israel' (5:8). But God was in control and he gave his people victory over their enemies.

Whatever is going on in our lives, God is working out his purposes. This is not always easy to see when we are in the middle of a problem or a crisis, but God's timing is perfect and we need to exercise patience and trust (see James 1:3-5).

A man on the run (4:17)

In the confusion of battle and the realization that escape by chariot was impossible, Sisera fled in the direction of Hazor, where his army had been based. The battle had been so intense that he could not manage the journey without rest and refreshment. Heber the Kenite had a settlement en route and it appears that he had a peace treaty with King Jabin, Sisera's master. This made the settlement a useful place for Sisera to stop and take some rest.

Earlier on in the chapter we are given an important detail about Heber—he was descended from Moses' brother-in-law (v. 11)! Also in 1:16 we are told that the Kenites settled in the south of Judah's territory, but Heber and his family separated from the rest and moved north. This is an important detail because it shows us how God was working all these things together to fulfil his purposes. Jabin had made a peace treaty with this powerful nomad for his own reasons, but he did not know that Heber came from a people-group who had strong links with the Israelites (which would have made him predisposed towards them). And Jael, Heber's wife, was in place to finish the battle by killing Sisera. This had already been prophesied by Deborah: when Barak said that he would put her God-given plan into action on the condition that she accompanied him Deborah said, 'Very well, I will go with you. But because of the way you are going about this, the honour will not be yours, for the LORD will hand Sisera over to a woman' (4:9).

Hammering the point home (4:18-23)

Sisera arrived at the settlement fatigued and famished, looking for food and shelter. He was oblivious to Jael's links with the Israelites and she appeared to be very hospitable and welcoming. 'Come, my lord, come right in,' she said. 'Don't be afraid' (v. 18). As far as Sisera was concerned he could not be safer. He was being sheltered by someone who had made a peace treaty with his master and was hiding in a woman's tent (which according to custom could not be searched). Jael covered Sisera with a flysheet to protect him from insects, gave him water and kept watch over his tent. And, just when he felt comfortable and secure, she struck: hammering a tent peg through his temple. It was a Kenite woman's responsibility to pitch tents and take them down when it was time to move on, so she would have been swift and accurate in her use of the tent peg; Sisera did not stand a chance of survival.

Deborah and Jael pose a striking contrast. One presents a soothing pastoral scene while the other provokes a shocking nightmare! Yet both are part of the drama of these chapters and are used by God to fulfil his purposes. And Deborah celebrates Jael's violent act in her song of praise (see 5:24-27).

A heartless woman?

So what should we make of Jael; was she a heartless murdering woman who became God's tool for justice? There is no doubting the fact that she was not a woman to be scorned! But faced with the choice of giving refuge to a man who murdered, raped and pillaged God's people or bringing his life to a swift end she chose an option that, in the long run, would be less violent. It is true that she lulled Sisera into a false sense of security, which does lay her open to the charge of being treacherous. But when faced with a choice, Jael sided with God's people and in doing so she was used by God to bring about their deliverance.

> These events are set in dark and violent times which called for desperate measures. Sisera was a ruthless man who lived by the sword and perished by the sword (see Matt. 26:52).

These events are set in dark and violent times which called for desperate measures. Sisera was a ruthless man who lived by the sword and perished by the sword (see Matt. 26:52). And Jael implemented some rough justice when it was in short supply. She brought a reign of terror to an end and that is why

Deborah rejoiced at her actions and called her 'most blessed of women' (5:24).

Perhaps we find passages like this difficult because we try to sanitize the Bible and smooth over the parts we are not comfortable with. Of course the events we have been thinking about do not call on Christian women to arm themselves with tent pegs! There is a significant shift of emphasis from the Old Testament to the New, because the Old focuses on a physical kingdom and the New on a spiritual one. But even in the New Testament there are still issues we might rather gloss over. We like to think of God's love and compassion but not about his judgement. We might enjoy talking to people about heaven, but not be so comfortable speaking about hell. These are not issues that our politically correct culture finds palatable, but they are addressed in the Bible and we must be faithful to what it says.

FOR FURTHER STUDY

1. Compare Deborah with Miriam (Exod. 15:20-21), another of the three women prophets in the Old Testament. Think about the way in which Deborah was able to have the victorious attitude displayed by Miriam, while her people were still suffering.

2. What aspects of Hebrews 11:38 are evident in the conduct of Deborah and Barak?

TO THINK ABOUT AND DISCUSS

1. After the people of Israel had forsaken the Lord, they appeared to be oblivious to the way in which their enemies the Canaanites had regrouped and become a threat. Think about times when your love for the Lord has grown cold. What kind of spiritual enemies have begun to reappear in your life?

2. Although the people of Israel were suffering great oppression, Deborah was able to bring wisdom and counsel to them. Think about the positive influence you could be in difficult situations at work, college or in your neighbourhood.

How can the church fulfil Jesus' command to be 'the salt of the earth' (Matt. 5:13)? Consider this in relation to social injustice and global poverty.

4 The man who made a difference

(6:1-32)

Another 'ever-decreasing circle' spawned a different enemy! The Midianites were an old adversary who had initially been defeated in the days when the Israelites lived in the desert under Moses' leadership (see Num. 31), but now, centuries later they had regrouped and become a formidable force.

They were very effective in waging war on both the physical and the psychological fronts. Their tactics were very different from those used by the Canaanites (described in the previous chapters); instead of invasion and conquest they chose to use a form of terrorism. The Israelites would be allowed to attend to their crops and maintain their livestock. And just at the crucial time, when the crops were ready to harvest and their livestock had become strong and healthy, the Midianites would launch an attack (see vv. 2-5).

The scope of their reign of terror expanded when they

made an alliance with the Amalekites and 'other eastern peoples' (v. 3). The Amalekites had attacked the people of Israel when they first left Egypt (see Exod. 17:8-16). And 'other eastern peoples' is a general description of people who came from the desert region to the east of the Promised Land.

Tell me the old, old story! (vv. 1-10)

We are not left in any doubt as to why all this had happened. At the very beginning of the chapter the writer tells us: 'Again the Israelites did evil in the eyes of the LORD' (v. 1). And after seven years of oppression and fear they finally called out to God for help. However, first they needed to listen to a word from God which was brought by an unnamed prophet. The Lord had heard their prayer and he already had his hand on the man he was going to use to deliver them, but first they had to understand the reason for their difficulties—they had forsaken God. The message began with a statement about the wonderful things God had done for the nation in the past (vv. 8-9). He had led them out of Egypt (whose rulers had oppressed their ancestors by putting them into slavery), driven their enemies out before them and given them the land they now lived in. He had told them that he was 'the Lord [their] God' and commanded them not to worship 'the gods of the Amorites'. But they had disobeyed him and worshipped other gods.

The Israelites had a unique relationship with God. The Bible describes it as a covenant, which is a 'divinely imposed legal agreement between God and man that stipulates the conditions of their relationship.'4 Shortly before the Israelites took possession of the Promised Land, Moses told them about the blessings they would receive if they kept their part of the covenant, by obeying God and being faithful to him (see Deut. 28:1-14). However, the consequences of forsaking the Lord were devastating: 'You will be unsuccessful in everything you do; day after day you will be oppressed and robbed, with no one to rescue you' (Deut. 28:29). This is an accurate description of what had happened to them at the hands of the Midianites.

It was not exactly the message the Israelites would have wanted to hear. They would have certainly preferred a reassuring promise that God was going to deliver them quickly! But it was important for them to be faced with the facts: they had forsaken the Lord and the oppression they were suffering was a direct consequence of this.

Handle with care!

We must be very careful in applying this to our own lives. It does not necessarily mean that difficulties and setbacks are consequences of disobedience to God. In fact the New Testament tells us that God allows trials to come into our lives in order to help us to mature (see James 1:2-4). However, we should develop the discipline of standing back, taking a careful look at what we are doing and asking ourselves whether some of the difficulties we face might be related to disobedience. We can make David's prayer our own and say,

Search me, O God, and know my heart;
test me and know my anxious thoughts.
See if there is any offensive way in me,
and lead me in the way everlasting
(Ps. 139:23-24).

An ordinary man (v.11)

Gideon is the central character in this particular 'ever-decreasing circle'. He lived in one of the most dispiriting times God's people had experienced; but his life was transformed when he met with God. He became a man who made a difference!

There was nothing particularly special about Gideon; he was an ordinary young man, from an inconsequential family. And he was living through a traumatic period in Israel's history, doing what he could to survive.

Gideon's home town, Ophrah, was near the border with Midian and it would have been the first place affected by the attacks. When we are introduced to him we find that he is threshing wheat in a winepress. This was an unusual thing to do; wheat was usually threshed on the floor of a barn while a winepress was used to

The New Testament tells us that God allows trials to come into our lives in order to help us to mature (see James 1:2-4). However, we should develop the discipline of standing back, taking a careful look at what we are doing and asking ourselves whether some of the difficulties we face might be related to disobedience.

crush grapes. But Gideon was using the winepress to hide the grain from the Midianites; the scene speaks of defeat and despair.

A heavenly visitor (vv. 11-16)

Gideon was being watched by someone who was going turn defeat into victory and despair into hope: 'The angel of the LORD came and sat down under the oak' (v. 11). This was a theophany (a visible manifestation of God). But not realizing the true identity of his visitor, Gideon was taken aback by the way he greeted him: 'The LORD is with you, mighty warrior' (v. 12). This led Gideon to unleash a stream of agonizing questions that he had been wrestling with. '"But sir," Gideon replied, "if the LORD is with us, why has all this happened to us? Where are all his wonders that our fathers told us about when they said, 'Did not the LORD bring us up out of Egypt?' But now the LORD has abandoned us and put us into the hand of Midian"' (v. 13).

Gideon had endured seven years of oppression meted out by the Midianites. He could not reconcile the great events of his people's history, such as the exodus from Egypt and their entry into the Promised Land, with the suffering they were enduring at the hands of their enemy. It is interesting that the angel of the Lord did not even address these questions, he just told Gideon to 'go in the strength [he had] and save Israel out of Midian's hand', adding the challenge, 'Am I not sending you?' (v. 14). Gideon seemed to be painfully aware of his shortcomings (v. 15). He was the weakest man, from the lowest family, of the smallest clan in the least significant tribe. But he was God's man and he was given the same promise that been given to Moses (see Exod. 3:12) and Joshua (see Josh. 1:5): 'I will be with you' (v. 16).

Strength for struggles

There will be times when we find ourselves in a similar position to Gideon; unable to reconcile the spiritual victories we read about in the Bible with the struggles we are going through. We may have agonizing questions to which there will be no answer this side of heaven. However, Jesus has given us the same promise that God had given to Gideon; he said: 'surely I will be with you always, to the very end of the age' (Matt. 28:20). If we grasp this, like Gideon, we will be people who make a difference. We do not have to be clever or influential; all that is necessary is that we are committed to Christ, obedient to his word and dependent on his strength. Remember that one of the most influential Christians who ever lived, the apostle Paul, said 'When I am weak, then I am strong' (2 Cor. 12:10).

The fear of the Lord (vv. 17-32)

When the heavenly visitor was presented with his food he touched it with the tip of his staff and 'fire flared from the rock, consuming the meat and the bread. And the angel of the LORD disappeared' (v. 21). Gideon's reaction was one of fear (v. 22). It was the kind of fear the Bible exhorts us to have: a deep reverence for God and a desire to please him. It brought words of assurance from the Lord (v. 23). And Gideon was motivated to obey God's command to tear down the altar that had been devoted to Baal, replacing it with 'a proper kind of altar to the LORD [his] God' (v. 26).

Although Gideon's actions initially provoked a huge outcry from the people of the town, his father's intervention made them see that he had done the right thing. This is all the more amazing as Joash, his father, was the patron of the shrine. Yet Gideon's bold action made Joash realize the worthlessness of the god they had been worshipping. 'If Baal really is a god,' he declared, 'he can defend himself when someone breaks down his altar' (v. 31). This persuaded the inhabitants of the town to support Gideon; they even gave him a new name, 'Jerub-Baal', which meant 'let Baal contend with him' (v. 32). Gideon was now in a strong position to lead them in the fight against their enemy.

We usually think of fear as something that should not be part of the Christian life and the New Testament tells us that 'perfect love drives out fear' (1 John 4:18). However, it is important that we have the right kind of fear—that which Gideon displayed—so that we set our sights on pleasing God, even if it brings us into conflict with people around us. We will find that he will honour this and use it to inspire other people to make a stand.

1. Read Deuteronomy 28. In what ways had Israel enjoyed the blessings of obedience to God? Compare the curses (v. 15-44) with the circumstances described in Judges 6:1-6.

2. The Lord tells Gideon to 'go in the strength [he has]' (Judg. 6:14). What is this strength (see 6:34; 7:2,7)? Compare this to Jesus' promises to the apostles (Acts 1:8) and think about the reasons why the Holy Spirit gave them power. What encouragement does this give us for the mission God has given us?

TO THINK ABOUT AND DISCUSS

1. When the Lord told Gideon that he was going to use him 'to save Israel out of Midian's hand' (6:14), he protested, 'My clan is the weakest in Manasseh, and I am the least in my family' (6:15). Think about the reasons you have given to resist a work the Lord has called you to, particularly things that reflect a lack of confidence in your own abilities. How could you use such apprehensions to your advantage (see 2 Cor. 12:10; 13:4)?

2. Proverbs 1:7 tells us that 'the fear of the LORD is the beginning of knowledge'. Take a moment to define this, and think about the difference this concept will make to your everyday life, particularly in the way you use your time, the choices you make, your conversation and the television programmes that you watch.

5 Let the battle commence!

(6:33-7:25)

The Midianites and their allies had crossed the river Jordan and camped out in the Valley of Jezreel to launch more raids on the Israelites. This valley stood at the junction of Asia, Africa and Europe and was the crossroads of the north of Israel. It was a crucial region to control because it provided a natural corridor between the Nile and the Euphrates.

A call to arms (6:33-35)

It was the eighth year in succession this had happened, but on this occasion things were going to unfold very differently, because God had raised up a new judge. This was highlighted by the way in which 'the Spirit of the LORD clothed Gideon' (v. 34, ESV). One commentator says, 'The Spirit of the LORD became incarnate in Gideon who then became an extension of the LORD.'5 The victory that was shortly to be achieved would be due to God's work, not Gideon's leadership.

Gideon blew a trumpet summoning people to stand up to the enemy. The Abiezrites, who were from Gideon's home town, rallied behind him and the tribe of Manasseh made a positive response to the message that had been sent out to them. People from the neighbouring tribes of Asher, Zebulun and Naphtali gathered to the cause (v. 34), and eventually 32,000 troops were mustered.[6]

'Give me a sign—or two!' (6:36-40)

When Gideon was alone he seemed to be unsure as to whether he could complete the task the Lord had given him. He asked God to confirm that he would 'save Israel by [his] hand as [he had] promised' (v. 36), by making some wool wet when the ground was dry. He left the wool out overnight and found there was enough dew in it to fill a bowl with water. But he was still not convinced, so he asked God to give him one more sign. This time he wanted the wool to be kept dry when the ground was wet. That would have been even more striking because wool naturally absorbs water. Again, Gideon left it overnight and he returned to find the fleece dry when the ground was wet with dew (v. 40). Some people have tried to do something similar when they have needed guidance from God; they have even described it as 'putting out a fleece'. For example, they might ask God to show them that it is right to take a job offer by sending a particular person to speak to them or making something happen. While their desire to do God's will is commendable, it is not right to use Gideon's actions as a template for guidance. The incident we read about here gives us an example of God's patience and kindness. Gideon had already been given the guidance he needed, but God looked on his uncertainty with compassion and reassured him. So instead of treating these verses as a pattern for guidance, we should see them as an example of God's care. There will be times when we become uncertain about a task God has called us to do and we should take encouragement from the way in which he cared for Gideon. 'As a father has compassion on his children, so the LORD has compassion on those who fear him; for he knows how we are formed, he remembers that we are dust' (Ps. 103:13-14).

Too many men (7:1-8)

It was a striking contrast. On one side of the Jordan were the Midianites and their allies, preparing to unleash another wave of destruction and terror on the Israelites. And on the other side was a collection of men from the northern tribes who did not have the numbers, experience, or the military hardware to match their enemy. But they had seen God's hand on Gideon, and were ready to follow him into battle.

Their leader was waiting for God to give the order to attack. But first there was an unexpected command. The Lord said to Gideon, 'You have too many men for me to deliver Midian into their hands. In order that Israel may not boast against me that her own strength has saved her...' (7:2). The Midianites already outnumbered them, and that was without taking into account the enormous military advantages they had in terms of equipment and experience. But God knew that unless it was patently obvious that he had delivered them the Israelites would take the credit themselves for the victory. And he was not going to share his glory with anyone, so the army had to be reduced. This was done in two phases. First, God told Gideon to allow anyone who was overcome with fear to walk away (see Deut. 20:8), and 22,000 men left. But that was not enough: 'The LORD said to Gideon, "There are still too many men. Take them down to the water, and I will sift them out for you there. If I say, 'This one shall go with you,' he shall go; but if I say, 'This one shall not go with you,' he shall not go'" (7:4). The men were taken down to the river to get a drink. Those who knelt down to drink were separated from those who lapped water; 9,700 were in the first group and 300 in the second. And the shocking news for Gideon was that the largest group had to leave, reducing his army to 300 men! We are not told why men who lapped the water were the ones who were to stay. Some people say this was because they would have been able to jump up at a second's notice and fight their enemy, thereby showing themselves to be more vigilant. But there is nothing in the text that suggests this might be the reason. It was God's way of reducing the army to a small number so that it would be clear that the victory was from him.

> There will often be times when God strips away the things or the people we lean on and brings us into situations in which we become very aware of our weaknesses.

There will often be times when God strips away the things or the people we lean on and brings us into situations in which we become very aware of our weaknesses. This makes us more dependent upon him and provides greater potential to glorify him.

More encouragement (7:9-15)

After reducing the ranks of his army, God sent Gideon to the enemy's camp and told him to listen to what they were saying. As a result he gained encouragement from the lips of one of the Midianites who was telling his friend about a dream he had: 'A round loaf of barley bread came tumbling into the Midianite camp. It struck the tent with such force that the tent overturned and collapsed' (v. 13). A barley loaf was associated with people who were poor and oppressed, and the Midianite's friend was in no doubt as to the significance of the dream: 'This can be nothing other than the sword of Gideon… God has given the Midianites and the whole camp into his hands.' Dreams were very significant to people living at this time, and there is no doubt that God brought about this one in order to encourage Gideon. As Spurgeon put it, 'God holds the brain of this sleeping Arab in his hand and impresses it as he pleases.'[7] It had the desired effect; Gideon worshipped the Lord and returned to base ready to face his enemy in God's strength.

God knows when we need encouragement and sometimes he will use the most unlikely people to bring it to us.

The first victory (7:15-25)

The tactics used to fight the Midianites were very unconventional. The men were divided into three groups of a hundred. Each man took a torch, a jar and a trumpet. The torches were flames, and they were to be put in earthenware jars which would have hidden the flames until they were smashed, while the trumpets were blown to cause confusion in the enemy's ranks. At Gideon's signal they were to blow their trumpets, smash the jars, wave the torches and shout 'a sword for the LORD and for Gideon'. These tactics caused so much confusion and panic among the enemy that they attacked one another by mistake. Three hundred men armed with torches and trumpets defeated the most formidable army of the day. The victory, though, was not theirs, but God's.

The New Testament tells us that we face a powerful and skilful enemy (see Eph. 6:10 ff.; 1 Peter 5:8). But we can fight him in the assurance that Christ has already won the victory (see Col. 2:15). We may feel small and outnumbered but, like Gideon and his army, the Lord is on our side and will lead us to victory.

FOR FURTHER STUDY

1. Apply Deuteronomy 8:17, Isaiah 10:13 and 2 Chronicles 10:15 to the situation the Israelites were in when they faced the Midianites.

2. Look at the way in which God uses the dream he gives to Nebuchadnezzar in Daniel. What does this tell us about the way in which God works out his purposes?

TO THINK ABOUT AND DISCUSS

1. Think about the way God may wean us from depending on things other than himself, particularly strength of numbers or finance.

2. Proverbs 21:1 says that 'the king's heart is in the hand of the LORD; he directs it like a watercourse wherever he pleases'. Consider the way in which God has used people who are not Christians to bring you to where he wants you to be. Can he use people who are hostile towards us (see Gen. 50:20; Ps. 76:10)?

6 The enemy within

(8:1-32)

At last the Midianites' grip on Israel had been loosened. Freedom and security were in sight. But another enemy was already emerging, one which was more subtle and dangerous than the Midianites—the enemy within!

Dissension defused (vv. 1-3)

The massive army that had gathered to launch an attack on Israel was in disarray. Gideon had sent out a message to three other tribes, Naphtali, Asher, and Manasseh. He had asked them to help the campaign by seizing the territory around the streams that flowed into the Jordan from the west. They made a quick response, capturing and killing Oreb and Zeeb, two Midianite captains. But when the Ephraimites met Gideon they were unhappy that he had not asked them to take part earlier in the campaign (v. 1). Gideon defused the situation by showing humility, giving them respect and redirecting their focus towards the Lord. 'He answered them, "What have I accomplished compared to you? Aren't the gleanings of Ephraim's grapes better than the full grape harvest of Abiezer? God gave Oreb and Zeeb, the Midianite leaders, into your hands. What was I able to do compared to you?" At this, their resentment against him subsided' (vv. 2-3).

It is very dispiriting when we find ourselves criticized by other Christians but Gideon gives us a positive example as to how we should handle it. Like him, we must have a humble attitude, show respect, speak to our critics calmly and remind them of the bigger work of which they are part.

Self-preservation (vv. 4-21)

The battle had been raging and the men were exhausted; they needed to stop and eat. When they arrived at a town called Succoth, which was about fifty miles away from the battleground, Gideon asked for some food for his men. But he did not get the response he had hoped for: 'Do you already have the hands of Zebah and Zalmunna in your possession? Why should we give bread to your troops?' (v. 6). Zebah and Zalmunna were Midianite kings, and the people of the town refused to be confident of Gideon's army's victory until these men were captured. They did not want to suffer reprisals from the Midianites if Gideon failed, so they thought it would be safer to refuse the request. The same pattern of events happened when Gideon and his men arrived at Peniel, a town that was five miles away.

Gideon warned the citizens of both towns of the consequence of their failure to support him in this practical way (vv. 7-9). When he returned, having captured the two men they had been pursuing, he went to Succoth, 'punishing them with desert thorns and briars' (v. 16). Then he visited Peniel to pull down their tower and kill some of their men.

These people refused to help Gideon out of self-preservation, but ironically they had put themselves in a more dangerous position because after Gideon had accomplished his mission, they faced the consequences of not standing with him. Jesus said, 'Whoever finds his life will lose it, and whoever loses his life for my sake will find it' (Matt. 10:39). There will be times when God will require us to make a stand for him and this will involve the risk of reprisals and suffering. But if we shrink from the challenge and try to protect ourselves we will pay the cost.

From victory to defeat (vv. 22-32)

Fresh from victory, and full of relief and gratitude, the Israelites invited Gideon to rule them. On the surface his response was commendable: 'I will not rule over you, nor will my son' (v. 23). However this was not quite what it seemed. Gideon appeared to enjoy being treated like a king. He had a harem (v. 30), he acquired the Midianites' royal jewellery (v. 26), and after he died his son, Abimelech assumed a position of leadership as if he were part of a dynasty (9:2). So, although Gideon's words seem to say one thing, it appears that they were designed to enable him to have all the trappings of royalty without taking the title of 'king' or 'ruler'. The timid boy from Ophrah had turned into a pretentious man.

Gideon followed up his cleverly worded reply to their request by asking each man to give him a gold ear-ring from their share of the plunder. The response was overwhelming and Gideon used the gold to make an ephod. This was a garment usually worn by the high priest. It was a sleeveless tunic, with a breastplate upon which twelve precious stones were mounted (representing the tribes of Israel). The ephod had a pouch to contain items known as Urim and Thummin, which were used to discern God's will. There is no doubting that God had given Gideon direct guidance in the past, but he was not to be an ongoing channel for it. Sadly he seemed to let the people's gratitude affect him so that he thought of himself 'more highly than [he] ought' (Rom. 12:3).

The end result was that the ephod was put on display and people began to worship it (v. 27). The man who led them out of oppression drew them back into idolatry.

We are at our most vulnerable to spiritual defeat when we have seen blessing and success. There is a danger that we can enjoy the attention people give us, and allow pride to creep in so that we put our focus on ourselves rather than on the Lord. The New Testament warns that 'if you think you are standing firm, be careful that you don't fall!' (1 Cor. 10:12). We must never be complacent about the enemy within.

FOR FURTHER STUDY

1. How does the way in which Gideon responds to the Ephraimites' complaint demonstrate the principles set out in Proverbs 15:1 and Colossians 3:12-14?

2. The story of Gideon ends on a tragic note with the Israelites being drawn back into idolatry by an object he had created. How could this have been avoided if he had been able to read the warnings contained in 1 Corinthians 10:12 and Proverbs 16:18?

TO THINK ABOUT AND DISCUSS

1. Think about areas of tension and conflict you may be caught up in at church, home or work. In what ways would you be able to take the same approach Gideon took with the Ephraimites?

2. The New Testament urges us to 'be self controlled and alert' because our enemy, Satan, 'prowls around like a roaring lion looking for someone to devour' (1 Peter 5:8). Which areas in your life are most prone to his attack and how can you 'resist him, standing firm in the faith' (1 Peter 5:9)? Think about weaknesses you have and how you could be placing yourself in spiritual danger.

7 Life without God

(8:33-9:57)

Now that God had given the Israelites peace and security, we would expect them to have a sense of gratitude. But tragically, that was not the case.

Back to Baal! (8:33-35)

The writer tells us that 'no sooner had Gideon died than the Israelites again prostituted themselves to the Baals. They set up Baal-Berith as their god and did not remember the Lord their God, who had rescued them from the hands of all their enemies on every side' (vv. 33-34). 'Baal-Berith' is a term used a number of times in this part of the book, meaning 'Baal of the covenant'. This is the same Canaanite idol they had been worshipping before God raised up Gideon, but it may have been described in this way because the people of Israel had made some kind of treaty with their pagan neighbours, who worshipped Baal, or because they had made a public commitment to the idol. Although we cannot be sure of the precise reason, it powerfully underlines the tragedy of these events. They had forsaken their covenant relationship with the Lord and had given themselves to Baal. They were prepared to call upon God in a time of crisis but when life returned to normal they once more rejected him and turned to Baal.

There is no doubting the fact that these people were very fickle in their relationship with God. However, before we condemn them, we should take a look at our own hearts and lives. In difficult times we turn to God and ask for his help, but once we are through them our hearts can grow cold and our commitment can weaken. We may not involve ourselves in a false religion, as the Israelites did, but we can allow our homes, or money, or sport, or pleasure to become the centre of our lives. When we do so these things become as much of an idol as Baal was to the Israelites.

A cunning coup (9:1-6)

In his latter years Gideon had adopted a regal lifestyle; he amassed great wealth, gathered a huge harem of wives for himself and fathered seventy sons. He also had a concubine (a woman with whom he had a physical relationship, but to whom he was not married). She was a slave girl from Shechem (a city that lay in the valley between mounts Ebal and Gerizim, thirty-four miles north of Jerusalem) and had a son by Gideon called Abimelech. After Gideon's death the sons he had by his wives appear to have formed some kind of collective government but Abimelech was not included. He saw this as an opportunity to seize power, and gathered together the relatives from his mother's side to put forward a plan. They were to ask the citizens of Shechem a loaded question: 'Which is better for you: to have all seventy of Jerub-Baal's [Gideon's] sons rule over you, or just one man?' Abimelech also added a reminder to them that he was their 'flesh and blood' (v. 2). As their relative he would be better placed to serve their interests and as Gideon's son he would be in a good position to seize power. The plan was successful; they gave Abimelech money from the treasury of Baal's temple and he used it to hire some mercenaries. Sixty-nine of his half brothers were murdered and the people of Shechem made him their king.

Time to choose (9:7-21)

Jotham, Gideon's youngest son, was able to hide from Abimelech's assassins and escape the slaughter. He kept a low profile until the day of the coronation. Just as the crowd fell silent and the king-elect was about to be crowned, Jotham called out from the mountain just above them. He probably would have been standing on a crag protruding from the mountain, which would have provided a natural platform and excellent acoustics. 'Listen to me citizens of Shechem,' he said, 'so that God may listen to you' (v. 7).

Jotham went on to tell a parable (vv. 8-15). The trees decided among themselves that it was time they had their own king. So they approached those that might be suitable. The olive tree, the fig tree and the vine all refused because they had more important functions to perform—those they were created for. But the thorn bush was interested, saying, 'If you really want to anoint me king over you, come and take refuge in my shade; but if not, then let fire come out of the thorn bush and consume the cedars of Lebanon!' (v. 15). The people who had been listening worked on the land and would have quickly understood the message of the parable. Thorn bushes provided fuel for fire, but they could never provide shelter. The people were about to do something as foolish as taking shelter under a thorn bush, and this particular variety would not only scratch them, it was going to catch fire and burn them!

Jotham followed up his story with a challenge: 'If then you have acted honourably and in good faith towards Jerub-Baal and his family today, may Abimelech be your joy, and may you be his, too! But if you have not, let fire come out from Abimelech and consume you, citizens of Shechem and Beth Millo, and let fire come out from you, citizens of Shechem and Beth Millo, and consume Abimelech!" (vv. 19-20). He knew that the second part of

> When people reject God they do not choose freedom; they place themselves under tyranny.

his challenge was correct. They had not acted honourably, and he was warning them of the consequences of placing themselves under the rule of a ruthless killer like Abimelech .

Centuries later a crowd of chief priests stood in front of Pilate and said, 'We have no king but Caesar' (John 19:15). Caesar was the very man whose rule they had longed to be free from, yet they were hailing him as their emperor. When people reject God they do not choose freedom; they place themselves under tyranny.

God is not mocked (9:22-57)

The people rejected Jotham's warning and made Abimelech king, but 'God is not mocked' (Gal. 6:7, ESV). The author leaves us in no doubt that the events which bring this tragic phase of Israel's history to a close came from God (see vv. 23-24, 56-57).

God caused conflict between Abimelech and the citizens of Shechem. They set up raiding parties to ambush passers-by and destabilize Abimelech's rule. A man called Gaal, described by Leon Wood as 'a sort of knight errant who moved through the country with a group of ... fellow knights to seize advantages and opportunities',[8] arrived on the scene. He won the hearts of the people of Shechem and used his influence to inflame even further feelings of discontent against Abimelech, so that he could put himself forward as the leader they had been waiting for (vv. 27-29). Abimelech's informant, Zebul, told him what had been happening and advised him to quell the rebellion by mobilizing his fighters and placing them in the fields under the cover of darkness. They were to lie in wait and attack Gaal and his men when they came out of the city in the morning (vv. 31-33). So Gaal was crushed by Abimelech's army and the next day, as the people left the city to go out to work in the fields, they were slaughtered. They then attacked the city itself and as a final insult they covered it in salt. Those who were left ran from the city to take refuge in the tower (that was part of Baal's temple) but Abimelech set fire to it killing a thousand people. After his success against the citizens of Shechem, Abimelech decided to attack the neighbouring town, Thebez. When he captured it, the people took refuge in a tower and Abimelech decided to use the same tactics he had employed earlier. But, as he reached the entrance, a women dropped a stone on his head and cracked his skull. To spare him the disgrace of being killed by a woman Abimelech told his servant to put him to death with his sword, and his death brought the conflict to an end.

No act of bloodshed goes unnoticed by God, no injustice will be left unpunished; he is 'the Judge of all the earth [who shall] do right' (Gen. 18:25).

For further study ▶

FOR FURTHER STUDY

1. In what way is the rule of Abimelech a foretaste of Saul's reign (see 1 Sam. 8)?

2. How does the attitude of the people, described in Judges 9:1-6, compare to that in 1 Samuel 8:19?

TO THINK ABOUT AND DISCUSS

1. Read Galatians 5:1 and identify any areas in your life where you could lose the freedom God has given you in Christ. Are you affected by legalism or becoming dominated by sin?

2. How does the principle of 'putting to death the deeds of the body' in Romans 8:11-14 help you to be free from the domination of sin? Think about practical ways you can do so, by refusing to engage in some practices and devoting yourself to wholesome things instead.

8 Watch your words!

(10:1-11:40)

As we move into another 'ever-decreasing circle' the writer gives a detailed description of the people's sin and faithlessness.

'Again the Israelites did evil in the eyes of the LORD. They served the Baals and the Ashtoreths, and the gods of Aram, the gods of Sidon, the gods of Moab, the gods of the Ammonites and the gods of the Philistines. And ... the Israelites forsook the LORD and no longer served him' (10:6).

The Ammonites were from the east of Gilead (the area where the action takes place), and the Philistines were from the west. They combined forces to attack Israel from two directions; the Ammonites occupied Gilead while the Philistines attacked from the west. The people reacted predictably; they cried out to God and said, 'We have sinned against you, forsaking our God and serving the Baals' (v. 10). But God's response was totally unexpected:

> When the Egyptians, the Amorites, the Ammonites, the
> Philistines, the Sidonians, the Amalekites and the Maonites

oppressed you and you cried to me for help, did I not save you from their hands? But you have forsaken me and served other gods, so I will no longer save you. Go and cry out to the gods you have chosen. Let them save you when you are in trouble! (vv. 11-14).

Words are a central theme in chapters 10-13, and those cried out by the Israelites in these verses were empty. They were not repentant that they had forsaken God; they were just troubled by the consequences of their sin. But God would not deliver them until they recognized his right to rule over their lives. And they needed to demonstrate their repentance by rejecting the idols they had been worshipping.

The New Testament tells us that when we confess our sins to God he is 'faithful and just and will forgive us our sins' (1 John 1:9). But we should never take God's promise of forgiveness for granted or abuse his grace. Repenting from sin requires the forsaking of sin. We must treat the subject of sin seriously.

Challenging words (10:17-11:11)

The people responded to the Lord's rebuke by getting rid of their idols. Meanwhile the Ammonites had sent extra troops into Gilead, a mountainous region east of the Jordan, to consolidate their position. But, since they had restored their relationship with God, the Israelites seemed to have a new confidence and they saw these latest events as an opportunity to confront their enemy. So they assembled at Mizpah and decided that whoever launched an attack against the enemy would become their leader (10:18).

Despised and rejected

At the beginning of chapter 11 we are given some important background information about Jephthah, the man who was going to become their leader. The first details suggest that he was suitable for the position; coming from Gilead and being a 'mighty warrior' (the Hebrew word speaks of great courage and natural leadership abilities). However, the other details would have caused many of his contemporaries to question his suitability to lead them. His mother was a prostitute. And it would appear that Jephthah was taken into his father's home. Eventually they drove him out and he moved north of Gilead to a place called Tob, where a group of outcasts—who were probably drawn by his leadership abilities—gathered around him. Some people have seen this in quite a negative light, portraying Jephthah as an outlaw who surrounded himself with unsavoury men. But if that were the case the people of Gilead would never have approached him in the first place. It is more likely that he had made raids on the Ammonites and this would have brought him to the attention of the elders of Gilead, who invited him to become their commander (11:6).

Jephthah, an outcast who had been despised and rejected by his half-brothers, was their prospective leader. God has a way of using the people we least expect. This should not surprise us because Jesus himself was 'despised and rejected' and became 'a man of sorrows... familiar with suffering' (Isa. 53:3).

A search for sincerity

Once again the theme of words comes into the narrative. Jephthah challenges the sincerity of their invitation, reminding them of their initial involvement in his rejection (v. 7). But they asked him again, and this time he agreed as long as certain conditions were met. He was concerned that their words had no substance so he made them formalize their commitment to him before the Lord (11:11).

We live in an age in which words are twisted to mean anything people want them to, but, as God's people, we must mean what we say. The New Testament tells us to be 'slow to speak' (James 1:19) which means that we must think very carefully about what we are going to say. Words are important to the Christian; instead of stretching and twisting the truth, as so many people around us do, we must be sincere (see 1 Cor. 4:1-2).

A diplomatic offensive (11:12-27)

Before he led the people of Gilead into battle, Jephthah sent a message to the king of Ammon asking why he had been attacking them. The king replied by saying that it was because the Israelites' ancestors had stolen the territory from them and he demanded that they 'give it back peaceably' (11:13). Jephthah challenged the validity of the king's accusation by reminding him that God driven out the *Amorites* not the *Ammonites* from the territory they now occupied (21-22). It was never their land in the first place. He then affirmed that God had given the land to the Israelites and challenged the Ammonites to take the land that their god, Chemosh, gave them (23-26). Of course, he was not endorsing the worship of Chemosh—he was mocking their idolatry. 'The living God has given us this land,' he was saying. 'You will have to be content with what your god has given you.'

There are many attacks launched against the Good News. It is time for us to challenge people's misconceptions and defend the truth. And we must not be intimidated by the futile arguments that people put up against the message of Jesus—we should go on the counter-offensive!

An unexpected greeting (11:28-40)

After the king of Ammon rejected Jephthah's diplomatic initiative the Israelite troops were mobilized. Before he led them into battle Jephthah vowed to God that whatever came out of the door of his house to meet him when he returned, victorious, would be sacrificed (to God) 'as a burnt offering' (v. 31).

We are given a very concise account of the battle because the writer wants to emphasize the consequences of Jephthah's vow. Dale Ralph Davis remarks that 'it is as if the writer wants to swallow up victory in sorrow.'9 When Jephthah arrived at his home, flushed with victory and full of joy, the first person he set his eyes on was his daughter. The writer describes this vividly, conveying the drama and tragedy of the occasion: 'When Jephthah returned to his home in Mizpah, who should come out to meet him but his daughter, dancing to the sound of tambourines! She was an only child. Except for her he had neither son nor daughter' (v. 34). In the shake of a tambourine, triumph turned to tragedy;

Jephthah was devastated: 'Oh! My daughter!' he exclaimed. 'You have made me miserable and wretched, because I have made a vow to the LORD that I cannot break' (v. 35).

A problem passage!

This must be one of the most troubling passages in the Old Testament. However, it may not be as bleak as we assume. There was nothing unusual about people making vows to God in Old Testament times. Jacob made a vow at Bethel, promising to dedicate a tenth of his property to the Lord if he would be with him (Gen. 28:1-22). Hannah vowed that if the Lord were to give her a son she would dedicate him to serving in the temple (1 Sam. 1:11). And David spoke of going to the temple to pay a vow that he had made to God in times of trouble (Ps. 22:25; 61:5-8). The problem, though, lies with the substance of Jephthah's vow and the fact that God allowed him to carry it through.

Many commentators have argued that, when Jephthah sacrificed his daughter 'as a burnt offering', he did not literally kill her but gave her to a life of service in the temple.[10] However, in recent years others have argued that he did end her life.[11] But the writer does not give us details of the young girl's death. He tells us that she told her father to 'do … just as [he] had promised' (v. 36). She requested that she be allowed to go out to the hills for two months to grieve over the fact that she would never marry (v. 37), and it became an annual custom for the young women to lament her (vv. 39-40). The last detail appears to be linked with the fact that she never married. The passage emphasizes that Jephthah's only daughter would never marry, which meant that his line would end. If we add to this the fact that Jephthah is listed among the faithful in Hebrews 11:32, it is very difficult to believe that he put her to death. One commentator says that the words of verse 39 'conceal more then they reveal'.[12]

An unnecessary promise

The point that gets lost in the arguments about whether or not Jephthah put his daughter to death is that he did not need to make such a vow. We are told that, after they removed their idols, God could 'bear Israel's misery no longer' (10:16). Immediately before the battle with the Ammonites God empowered Jephthah with his Spirit (11:29); he did not require him to make a vow, it was something Jephthah had added and it cost him dearly. Many other people have followed in his footsteps: the Pharisees, who added their own rules and regulations to the law, and false teachers who had slipped into the church, demanding that Gentile believers be circumcised (Gal. 5:1-12, Acts 15). There were also the people of the Middle Ages who did penance and paid for indulgences in the belief that these acts would bring them God's favour. And we can also adopt the same mindset when we think that God accepts us on the grounds of what we do for him rather than what he has done for us in Christ.

For further study ▶

FOR FURTHER STUDY

1. What are the similarities between God's response to the Israelites' prayer in 10:11-16 and the rebuke given through the prophet in Isaiah 1:10-20? Identify the factors that were lacking in their prayer (Judg. 10:10).

2. What do Proverbs 13:3, Ephesians 5:6 and Titus 2:8 tell us about the significance of the words that we speak?

TO THINK ABOUT AND DISCUSS

1. Think about things that you have said to people during the past day. How many of the words you have spoken were empty or destructive? Consider how you can use your speech to build people up.

2. How careful should you be about volunteering for a task? Should you hesitate to respond until you know that you can fulfil the commitment? Consider this in relation to activities in your church you would like to get involved in. How should this affect the way in which people are recruited for activities like Sunday school, door-to-door work or cleaning the church building?

9 The war of words

There is a song, made famous by Fred Astaire, which is all about the different ways we speak: 'You like potato and I like potaeto, you like tomato and I like tomaeto; potato, potaeto, tomato, tomaeto! Let's call the whole thing off!'

These lyrics are very amusing but they also make an important point: the way we pronounce a particular word reveals a lot about us and highlights the differences between people from different parts of a country. In Jephthah's time the way someone spoke the word 'Shibboleth' made a distinction between two people-groups and resulted in wholesale slaughter.

Sibling rivalry (v. 1)

After focusing on a tragic personal episode in Jephthah's life, the writer returns to national events. Men belonging to the tribe of Ephraim were so angry that they were not included in the battle with the Ammonites they wanted to 'burn down [Jephthah's] house over [his] head'. This was not an impulsive expression of anger; it had boiled over from resentment that had been nursed for generations. Gilead (Jephthah's home turf) was part of the territory belonging to the half-tribe of Manasseh. They were called a half-tribe because Joseph's sons, Manasseh and Ephraim, took the place of Reuben (one of Jacob's sons) as joint heads of one of the twelve tribes, so each was known as a 'half-tribe' (see Gen. 48 and 1 Chron. 5:1-2).

When Jacob laid hands on them, to symbolize their appointment and pronounce his blessing upon them, he put his right hand upon Ephraim, the younger of the two. In doing so he was effectively saying that Ephraim would have the larger portion of blessing. When their father, Joseph, tried to correct him, Jacob said 'I know, my son, I know. He [Manasseh] too will become a people, and he too will become great. Nevertheless, his younger brother will be greater than he, and his descendants will become a group of nations' (Gen. 48:19). As the families grew into tribes a great rivalry existed between them. We have already seen this in the last 'ever-decreasing circle', when the Ephraimites complained that Gideon (who was from the tribe of Manasseh) had not included them in his campaign against the Midianites (see 8:1). Now a fugitive from Gilead had become a judge in their region and had defeated the Ammonites without their assistance.

Setting the record straight (vv. 2-3)

Jephthah dealt with their grievance, arguing his case with

great clarity. He told them that the war with the Ammonites was not a pursuit of glory but a matter of national survival: 'I and my people were engaged in a great struggle' (v. 2a). He reminded them that he had invited the Ephraimites to join the 'struggle' but they refused: 'Although I called, you didn't save me out of their hands' (v. 2b). And he affirmed the fact that the Lord had given them the victory and challenged their attitude towards him: 'Now why have you come up today to fight me?'

This response has been contrasted with the way in which Gideon spoke to the Ephraimites (see 8:1-2). However, Jephthah did not merely have to deal with complaints; he also had death threats issued against him. There was also a hidden agenda behind their intimidation; they were trying to regain their primacy over the half-tribe of Manasseh.

There will be times when we must lovingly, but clearly, challenge people who come to us with objections and arguments. I have been a pastor for many years and in that time people have come to me, with a complaint, claiming that they represent 'a groundswell of opinion'. My response has been to say that while I am very happy to talk to them and interested in their opinions, they speak for themselves. When I have asked them to tell me who is involved in this 'groundswell' it has usually been limited to their own family and one or two close friends.

A word that divides (vv. 4-15)

The tension erupted into violence. The Ephraimites had called the people of Gilead 'renegades from Ephraim and Manasseh' (v. 4), meaning that they were the worthless refuse of the two half-tribes. When the people of Gilead mobilized their army, hostilities broke out and the Ephraimites suffered heavy losses. In the face of defeat they ran away but they were cut off at the ford of Jabbok, which stood between the two territories. This set the scene for a bloodbath, which had not been sanctioned by Jephthah. Everyone passing over the ford was asked to say the word 'Shibboleth'. This was pronounced differently by the two tribes and it enabled the Gileadites to discern who was from Ephraim and put them to death. As a result 42,000 people were slaughtered, a strong tribe was decimated and the nation was weakened. It all began with angry words expressing long-held resentments.

A solemn warning

It is always sad to hear news of a church that has become divided or of Christians who have broken fellowship because of personal differences. Although these things may seem to happen suddenly they have usually been fuelled by many months, or even years, of resentment, jealousy or unforgiving attitudes. Angry words usually have deep roots. Jealousy will turn to resentment and generate conflict. A lack of forgiveness will create a 'bitter root' which 'grows up to cause trouble and defile many' (Heb. 12:15). We should take careful note of three important principles given in the New Testament. Firstly, in James we are told that 'man's anger does not bring about the righteous life that God desires' (James 1:20). Secondly, Paul tells us that we must not allow 'the sun [to] go down while [we] are still angry' (Eph. 4:26). Thirdly, James warns us that 'where [we] have envy and selfish ambition, there [we] find disorder and every evil practice' (James 3:16).

FOR FURTHER STUDY

1. Look up Acts 15:36-41. Was Paul right to divide from Barnabas?
2. What were the roots of the division in Corinth (see 1 Cor. 1:10-17)? How would the teaching given in 1 Corinthians 13 resolve it?

TO THINK ABOUT AND DISCUSS

1. Are there times when division between Christians is unavoidable and even necessary? Think about it in the context of differences over doctrine and church practice. What should be the basis of Christian unity and the criteria for issues over which Christians divide?

2. Are there divisions and tensions in your church arising from differences of personality, class or culture? What positive things can you do to help defuse them?

10 A woman after God's heart

(13:1-25)

In Judges 13 we meet Manoah and his anonymous wife who become Samson's parents. They are contrasted with each other throughout the chapter.

The smallest circle

We have come to the last 'ever-decreasing circle'. The Lord had given the Israelites into the hands of the Philistines. They were the fiercest enemy they had faced yet, and this particular conflict stretches right back to the days of Joshua and projects forward to the reign of David, when they were finally defeated.[14]

A difficult existence (vv. 1-5)

Manoah and his wife lived in a place called Zorah, which was about two miles from the known border of Philistine territory. They would have had a tense, dangerous existence because they lived so close to the enemy and this would have been compounded by their personal sadness. Several times the narrator tells us that Manoah's wife was 'sterile and remained childless' (vv. 2-3). However, the Lord visited her in the form of an angel, addressing her personal tragedy and the nation's problems together, telling her that she was going to have a son who would 'begin [Israel's] deliverance' from the Philistines (v. 5).

Specific instructions

The Lord told Manoah's wife that her son was to be 'a Nazirite, set apart to God from birth' (v. 3) and because of this a razor was never to touch his head and he was not to drink alcohol. Nazirites were men who had consecrated themselves to the Lord for a specific period of time (see Num. 6). But Manoah's son was different; his consecration began as soon as he was born and was to last for the whole of his life.

A focus on God (v. 6)

Manoah was not with his wife when she encountered the Lord, and when she told him what had happened she emphasized the fact that this visitor had come from God. 'A man of God came to me,' she said. 'He looked like an angel of God, very awesome' (v. 6). She did not realize that her visitor was the Lord himself but she perceived that there was a sense of God's presence with him.

'More details please!' (vv. 7-14)

Manoah's wife passed on the instructions word for word; but this was not sufficient for her husband. He asked the Lord to send the 'man of God' to them again, to teach them how to bring up their child (v. 8). His prayer was answered, but not in the way he would have wanted; the Lord appeared to Manoah's wife while Manoah was working in the fields. She hurried to fetch him and when he met the angel he got straight to the practicalities, asking 'What is to be the rule for the boy's life and work?' (v. 12). However, the answer was a repetition of the initial instructions the angel had given his wife. Manoah wanted a manual on how to parent a judge, when all that he needed for now were the simple instructions his wife had already been given.

Day by day

We would often like God to give us more details about what he wants us to do in the future, but he normally leads us forward on a day by day basis. Jesus said, 'Sufficient for the day is its own trouble' (Matt. 6:34, ESV). We may not know what God wants us to do next year or the year after, but we do know, from his Word, what he requires us to do today. Let us get on with putting his Word into practice today and leave the future in his hands.

A slow realization (vv. 15-21)

Manoah appears to be a practical man who carefully observed social conventions, so he offered his visitor a meal. This was a very sensible practice because people travelled long distances and did not know how long it would be before they would be able to find somewhere to eat. But he did not realize that he was inviting the Lord himself for a meal! Manoah wanted to cook a young goat, but the invitation was not accepted. 'Even though you detain me,' the Lord said, 'I will not eat any of your food. But if you prepare a burnt offering, offer it to the LORD' (v. 16). This should have made Manoah think: his visitor was asking for a sacrifice to be offered rather than a meal prepared because he was God himself. That is why the writer adds the comment 'Manoah did not realize that it was the angel of the LORD' (v. 16). Not understanding the significance of this statement, Manoah asked his visitor's name 'so that we may honour you when your word comes true.' He was given another indication of the angel's identity when he replied, 'Why do you ask my name? It is beyond understanding.' The Hebrew word used here means 'separate' or 'surpassing' and it was used in this instance to help Manoah realize that he was speaking to God. However, it did not seem to register with him and, in keeping with the Lord's request, he presented the goat as a sacrifice. This is communicated to us in quite a matter-of-fact way, but suddenly the tone changes as the writer tells us that 'the LORD did an amazing thing while Manoah and his wife watched' (v. 19). The Hebrew word translated 'an amazing thing' was used in the Psalms to describe phenomenal acts of God—and this is one of them! God, manifesting himself in the form of this angel, revealed his true identity and Manoah finally realized that he was meeting with God! (v. 21).

> We would often like God to give us more details about what he wants us to do in the future, but he normally leads us forward on a day by day basis.

A down-to-earth God

The fact that it took Manoah so long to understand his visitor's true identity tells us that there was nothing about the Lord's appearance that suggested who he really was. Although this was a theophany (a visible manifestation of God), he came in the form of an ordinary person. When Jesus came to this world, not only did he become a human being (while still being God), but he took 'the very nature of a servant' (Phil. 2:7). John's Gospel tells us that 'he was in the world, and though the world was made through him, the world did not recognize him' (John 1:10).

There are times when we do not realize that God is meeting with us, for example when he sends trials and difficulties into our lives to help us to mature (James 1:3-4), or when he puts people into our lives whom he wants us to help (see Matt. 25:37-40).

Two reactions (vv. 22-25)

Manoah and his wife have been contrasted throughout the chapter, and this continues with their reaction to the revelation of God. While Manoah says, 'We are doomed to die... We have seen God!' (v. 22), his wife argues that if that were so, the Lord would not have accepted their offering. It is true that both react with fear, but Manoah's fear is focused on his own safety while his wife had the 'fear of the LORD', which is 'the beginning of wisdom' (Prov. 9:10). She took comfort from the fact that God had accepted their sacrifice and had given them instructions as to how they must bring up their son.

Two sources of comfort

We need to have an attitude of reverence towards God; but it must always be balanced with these two sources of comfort. Firstly, God receives us because he has accepted a sacrifice, although now it is not a young goat, as it was for Manoah and his wife, but the death of his Son. And secondly, he has spoken to us in his Word. A bumper sticker I once saw in America said it all: 'God said it, I believe it, that's sufficient!'

For further study ▶

FOR FURTHER STUDY

1. Look at Judges 6:11-24 and Exodus 3:1-14, and list the similarities and differences between the two accounts. What do they teach us about God?
2. What does Numbers 6:1-21 tell us about the purpose and requirements of a Nazirite vow?

TO THINK ABOUT AND DISCUSS

1. Spend some time considering your prayer life. Is it centred on your own needs and the practicalities of day-to-day living? How can it be more God-centred?
2. Do you like to have the details of your life planned out? Think about the way in which this may conflict with Jesus' teaching in Matthew 6:34. How could you change?

11 A man full of flaws

(14:1-15:20)

After a short spell on the mountain-top we are brought down to earth with a bump! The last detail we were given about Samson, the unborn judge, was that 'the Spirit of the LORD began to stir in him' (13:25). This would lead us to expect him to be a clear-thinking, clean-living servant of God.

However, such expectations are shattered by the man we meet in the chapters that follow. Samson seems to be a carnal rather than spiritual man: he has a weakness for women and a problem with uncontrolled anger. Yet God had chosen him to be a judge before he was born. Samson's failings help us to focus upon God's faithfulness. He is at work in spite of Samson rather than because of him, and he does this in the most unexpected ways through this unlikely servant.

God's purpose and Samson's plans (vv. 1-4)

Having giving us a detailed account of the way in which Samson's parents learned about his birth and how they should bring up their son, the writer takes us straight to Samson's adult life. Samson had visited Timnah, a town which was four miles west of his home. It was originally occupied by the tribe of Dan but was now populated and controlled by the Philistines. When he returned from Timnah he told his parents that he had seen a woman he wanted to marry. His parents would have known that it was forbidden to marry someone from a different race (Deut. 7:3-4). They tried to persuade him to find a wife from among his own people but he insisted that they 'get her for [him]' because she was 'right in [his] eyes' (v. 3, ESV; cf. 21:25).

After describing this scene of family tension, the writer tells us something that Manoah and his wife were not aware of: 'This was from the LORD, who was seeking an occasion to confront the Philistines' (v. 4). This verse is the key to understanding the whole chapter. It does not mean that Samson's behaviour was right but it does tell us that God was in control, using Samson's wilfulness to work out his purposes.

Preparation for confrontation (14:5-7)

Giving into Samson's wishes, his parents accompanied him to Timnah, apparently to make arrangements for the wedding. At some point in the journey Samson was separated from them and he encountered a young lion, which he 'tore ... apart with his bare hands' (v. 6). Many people have an image of Samson as some kind of muscleman, but the text tells us that he was able to win the fight with such ease because 'the Spirit of the LORD came upon him in power'. The original language carries the idea of the strength coming upon him very quickly so that he would have been in no doubt that it was from God; and this also happened on several other occasions (see 15:4-5,8; 16:3). We have already identified verse 4 as a key to understanding the passage and it helps us to realize that there was a purpose behind this event: God was making Samson aware of the strength he would be given when he was to take his stand against the Philistines.

A weakness emerges (14:8-17)

After making arrangements for the wedding Samson and his parents returned to Timnah. He became separated from them again and discovered that a swarm of bees had made a hive in the carcass of the dead lion. Samson scooped out some of the honey and handed it to his parents without telling them where it had come from (v. 9). This detail provides us with the background for his confrontation with the Philistines at the wedding feast.

It may have been the Philistines' custom to hold a big wedding feast after which the marriage would be made official and consummated. The bridegroom would usually invite companions to the feast but, since Samson was a Jew, the Philistines decided to provide him with thirty of their own people. During the festive atmosphere Samson challenged them to solve a riddle: 'Out of the eater, something to eat; out of the strong, something sweet' (v. 14). If they were able to answer within seven days he would give them 'thirty linen garments and thirty sets of clothes' (v. 13), and if not, they had to do the same for him. Riddles were a popular form of entertainment and they would have often been used at wedding feasts. However, this riddle was one-sided because only Samson would have known the answer. After spending three days trying to work out the solution the men at the feast threatened Samson's wife, telling her that if she did not 'coax' the answer from him they would incinerate her father and herself (v. 15). The Hebrew word for 'coax' is the same one used to describe the way in which Delilah later 'lured' Samson into telling her the secret of his strength (16:5).

> In many ways the life of Samson serves as a warning to us; he is everything a servant of God should *not* be. The writer has already shown us the potential of this man when the Spirit came upon him so that he could tear the lion apart with his bare hands.

Under the pressure of this macabre threat the young lady used tears and emotional blackmail to get the answer to the riddle (v. 16). At first he would not tell her, but after four days of relentless weeping and nagging he finally gave in 'because she continued to press him' (v. 17). Samson's weakness was already emerging.

In many ways the life of Samson serves as a warning to us; he is everything a servant of God should *not* be. The writer has already shown us the potential of this man when the

Spirit came upon him so that he could tear the lion apart with his bare hands. But now his weakness is revealed. If only he had exercised some of the self-discipline he learned from his Nazirite vows; women would never have been his downfall and his life would not have ended so tragically.

During the winter a town in Alaska looks like a scene from a Christmas card. But in the summer the gardens that were carpeted with a blanket of snow become littered with debris. Visitors may think that the people who live there wait until winter is over before they put these unsightly objects out. In fact they are always there, but during the big freeze they get buried by the snow. There is a danger that we try and hide our weaknesses and pretend they do not exist but, like the rubbish in those gardens, they will eventually come to the fore. It is better to face up to them and deal with them now. If Samson had woken up to what was happening to him and thought about how he could avoid such compromise in the future, his life and ministry would have ended very differently indeed.

The confrontation (14:18-20)

On the last day of the feast the Philistines gave Samson the answer to his riddle. Realizing what they had done he said: 'If you had not ploughed with my heifer, you would not have solved my riddle' (v. 18). This set the scene for the conflict which God had planned. And when the 'Spirit of the LORD came upon him in power' (v. 19) he went to Ashkelon, a coastal town twenty-three miles from Timnah which was one of the five main Philistine cities.[15] He killed thirty men, gave their clothes to the men who had given him the answer to his riddle and went back to his home. The contrast is striking: the Spirit of the Lord gave Samson a 'sudden accession of irresistible strength'[16] but he returned home 'burning with anger' (v. 19). God was using Samson in spite of his failings, not because of his faithfulness.

The Old Testament is often described as an anticipation of Jesus, but we might look at Samson and wonder how he would fit in with this. The answer is that his life was a contrast to that of Jesus. While the Spirit of the Lord 'rushed' on Samson and was with him for a limited time, he came upon Jesus, taking the form of a dove and remained on him (see Matt. 3:13-17; Luke 4:16-21). We follow in the footsteps of someone who is the direct opposite to Samson and he sends the Holy Spirit to enable us to live for him.

A one-man army (15:1a)

Sometime after he had stormed back to his father's house, Samson's thoughts returned to his wife. We are not told how long he had been away but we know that it would have been May or June when he returned, since it was the time of the wheat harvest. So, on a summer's day, Samson took the short journey to his wife's home town, looking forward to sleeping with her.

A vicious cycle (15:1b-8)

When Samson's father-in-law greeted him he said that he had given his daughter to Samson's friend. He was probably using the term 'friend' quite loosely and was referring to one of the Philistines who had been at the feast. On hearing this Samson said, 'This time I have a right to get even with the Philistines; I will really harm them' (v. 3). He used a word that spoke of innocence or blamelessness because he considered that he had just cause to attack them. But although he had a genuine grievance he seemed to be more interested in personal vengeance than concern for God's glory.

Samson took his revenge using an unusual but ingenious method. He caught 300 foxes, tied them in pairs by their tails, fastened a torch to every pair of tails and sent them out to burn up the Philistines' crops and olive groves. Coming at the peak of the harvest this would have been devastating and they were so angry that they burned Samson's wife and her father to death. This led to more violence, with Samson launching himself into an all-out assault and killing many of them
(v. 8).

These events should be understood in the light of the statement in 14:4: 'This was from the LORD, who was seeking an occasion to confront the Philistines'. However, we must also remember that God was using Samson in spite of his failings, not because of his faithfulness. His actions served to intensify a cycle of violence with a devastating outcome for his wife and father-in-law. We can look at his actions and thank God that he is able to use anyone to further his purposes; but when it comes to our own lives we must seek to follow another example—Jesus.

Peter tells us that '"he committed no sin, and no deceit was found in his mouth." When they hurled their insults at him, he did not retaliate; when he suffered, he made no threats. Instead, he entrusted himself to him who judges justly' (1 Peter 2:22-23).

No support from home (15:9-15)

The Philistines camped at Lehi (a place in Judah that would have been near the border with Philistia) and demanded that the Israelites hand Samson over to them (v. 9). The Israelites were so unnerved by this that they sent 3,000 men to ask Samson to surrender. 'Don't you realize that the Philistines are rulers over us?' they said. 'What have you done to us?' (v. 11). Considering that they had been oppressed by the Philistines for so many years it was an appalling statement but it was characteristic of an age when 'everyone did as he saw fit' (21:25). Their primary goal was to survive and they thought that their best chance lay in extraditing Samson, rather than rallying around him to fight their enemy.

While it is wonderful to have support and encouragement from God's people there will be times when their behaviour will disappoint us. Jesus experienced this when Peter denied that he ever knew him, and Paul spoke of a time when 'no one came to [his] support but everyone deserted [him]', although he was able to conclude that 'the Lord stood at [his] side' (2 Tim. 4:16-17).

Some people have argued that Samson began to behave more like a judge at this point. But his statement 'I merely did to them what they did to me' (v. 11) seems to rule out this idea. He still appeared to perceive his circumstances as a personal conflict with the Philistines and not a battle God had called him to fight. If he was beginning to take his responsibility seriously he would have challenged the Israelites to stand firm and trust in the Lord's strength, which he had seen at work in his own life. However, on the positive side, he did have a measure of faith and he must have known that God would give him the strength he needed to fight the Philistines. So he decided to agree to let them tie him up and hand him over to their enemy, and to use this as an opportunity to attack them again. While the motives and actions of Samson and his people are not what they should be, God overruled them, using the events that followed to fulfil his purposes. 'As he approached Lehi, the Philistines came towards him shouting. The Spirit of the LORD came upon him in power. The ropes on his arms became like charred flax, and the bindings dropped from his hands. Finding a fresh jaw-bone of a donkey, he grabbed it and struck down a thousand men'(vv. 14-15).

A one-man celebration (15:16-17)

Fresh from his victory, and probably fuelled by adrenaline, Samson made up a song:

> With a donkey's jaw-bone
> I have made donkeys of them.
> With a donkey's jaw-bone
> I have killed a thousand men
> (v. 16).

In the original language two of the words are almost identical; one translation catches the spirit of the song by putting it this way:

> With a jaw-bone of an ass
> I have piled them in a mass.[17]

Pithy and punchy as it was, this song had little chance of being included in the Psalms, because it was all about Samson with no mention of God. It was time for him to be reminded that he was a mere human being who could do nothing without God.

The place of dependence (15:18-20)

When the battle was over and the crowd had dispersed, Samson was alone. And as soon as his elation had waned he became acutely aware of his own needs. Although the Spirit of the Lord had descended upon him the fight would have taken a lot of physical and emotional energy from him. For the first time in the narrative, we hear him express a sense of weakness, saying, 'You have given your servant this great victory. Must I now die of thirst and fall into the hands of the uncircumcised?' (v. 18). And God was gracious, meeting Samson's need by providing him with the water he needed to sustain himself (v. 19).

There will be times when we feel totally drained and ready to give up. But this will serve to remind us of our own limitations and make us depend on God. That was Paul's experience when he asked God, three times, to take away a 'thorn in the flesh' that had been troubling him. The answer he was given was: 'My grace is sufficient for you, for my power is made perfect in weakness' (2 Cor. 12:9).

FOR FURTHER STUDY

1. We are told that, when Samson told his parents to make the necessary arrangements for him to marry a Philistine woman, 'they did not know that this was from the Lord' (14:4). Read Mark 14:1-2,10-11; Luke 22:1-6; John 17:12 and think about the way in which God used Judas' wrong intentions to bring about his purposes.

2. Samson's weakness for women begins to emerge in Judges 14. What do 1 Corinthians 9:24-27 and 1 Timothy 6:12 tell us about the way in which self-discipline can help us to overcome our weaknesses?

TO THINK ABOUT AND DISCUSS

1. Samson's encounter with the lion made him aware of the strength God had given him. What does God use to make us aware of the power he provides? Read 2 Corinthians 12:7-10 and think about this in relation to difficulties and disappointments you have faced.

2. Are there weaknesses in your life that you have left unchecked? Spend a few minutes listing them and thinking about steps you need to take to guard against the temptations they may lead you into.

12 The fall of a fool

(16:1-31)

We now fast-forward twenty years, where we see a familiar weakness creep back into Samson's life.

He went to Gaza, the most southerly of the five main Philistine cities, and while he was there he spent the night with a woman (v. 1). The wording seems to be designed to remind us of an earlier encounter: when he went down to Timnah and 'saw there a young Philistine woman' he wanted to marry (14:1). This time it was far worse—he had set his eyes on a prostitute. During the intervening twenty years Samson seemed to have learned little from his earlier experience and had become very careless, following his own desires, despite the danger into which it put him.

A close shave (vv. 1-3)

When news spread that Samson was in town men surrounded his house, ready to kill him at first light. But he left in the middle of the night and crept through the city as its inhabitants slept. When he arrived at the city gate it was locked, so he carried it away, along with the lock bar and the post, putting them on display on a hill. This gesture was a statement of defiance, declaring that the Philistines could never defeat or capture him. But he did not appear to consider that he had only been able to break out of the city because God had given him the strength to do so. He seemed oblivious to the danger that he had put himself into because he had been so reckless. As far as he was concerned he was a man whom God had endowed with great strength; nothing could stand in his way. This was a very dangerous attitude which eventually led to his tragic fall.

In the New Testament, Paul draws on the failings of the people of Israel while they were in the wilderness and warns us: 'If you think you are standing firm, be careful that you don't fall' (1 Cor. 10:12). Spiritual and moral carelessness begins with an attitude that says 'it could never happen to me'. It will lead us to toy with temptation which will result in sin. Blessings from God and success in our work for him do not make us immune from temptation and spiritual danger. We have a cunning enemy and a fallen nature and we must be diligent to make sure that we 'live by the Spirit' and do not 'gratify the desires of the sinful nature' (Gal. 5:16). If our desires are left unchecked Satan will do everything he can to lure us away from the Lord. However, God has given us his power which provides 'everything we need for life and godliness' (2 Peter 1:3).

My, my, my Delilah! (vv. 4-21)

Oblivious to the peril he had put himself into, Samson met

another woman, and this time she did not just ignite his desire, she captivated his heart. We are not told a great deal about her but—in view of her relationship with Samson's captors—we can assume that she was a Philistine. Delilah was the weapon they had been waiting for!

Secrets and lies

The tragic circumstances we read about in these verses follow a similar pattern to events surrounding Samson's wedding. The Philistines asked her to 'lure' Samson (the same Hebrew word as the one translated 'coax' in 14:15) into sharing his secret. However, this time the secret was not the answer to a riddle but the source of his strength (v. 5).

When I was young I was given a children's Bible. It had a picture of Samson which made him look like a muscleman! If this were true, the secret of his strength would have been obvious, but the Philistines' request to Delilah shows us that there was nothing about his physical appearance that would have suggested that he had great strength. It came from the Lord.

As soon as Samson made his next visit to Delilah she got to work on him, asking him to tell her 'the secret of [his] great strength and how [he could] be tied up and subdued' (v. 7). Samson seemed to treat it as a game, telling her that 'if anyone [tied him] with seven fresh thongs that have not been dried, [he would] become as weak any other man' (v. 7). After he had fallen into a deep sleep in Delilah's arms, the Philistines crept into his room, tied him up and lay in wait for him. Delilah woke Samson by saying that the Philistines were about to attack him, 'but he snapped the thongs as easily as a piece of string snaps when it comes close to a flame' (v. 9). Sounding remarkably like Samson's Philistine wife (see 14:16), Delilah continued to put pressure on him to reveal his secret.

Once again he lied and said that 'if anyone [tied him] securely with new ropes that have never been used, [he would] become as weak as any other man' (v. 11). She secured him with the ropes as he slept and once again falsely warned him that the Philistines were 'upon [him]'. 'But he snapped the ropes off his arms as if they were threads' (v. 12).

Delilah tried again, using the same tactics, and this time Samson told her, 'If you weave the seven braids of my head into the fabric on the loom and tighten it with the pin, I'll become as weak as any other man' (v. 13). Once again she woke him saying, 'The Philistines are upon you!' and when he awoke 'he pulled up the pin and the loom, with the fabric' (v. 14).

We are not told whether Samson was aware of the danger he was in, but when a man's hormones rule his life his brain becomes disengaged. Leon Wood comments that 'one cannot help but wonder at the unbelievable credulity and stupidity of Samson in not recognizing the true intent of the woman.'[18] Delilah did not give up, nagging him 'until he was tired to death' (v. 16). The Hebrew word used here also means 'to shorten', suggesting that she wore his defences down until he had no fight left in him. Eventually he gave her the information she wanted: 'No razor has ever been used on my head…because I have been a Nazirite set apart to God since birth. If my head were shaved, my strength would leave me, and I would become as weak as any other man' (v. 17). He fell asleep on Delilah's lap and she called a man to shave off seven braids of his hair; when she called out, 'The Philistines are upon you!' he assumed that he would be able to break free as

> There is a danger that, like Samson, we can toy with temptation, pushing the boundaries of what is acceptable as far as we can.

before, 'but he did not know that the LORD had left him'. His infatuation had led to betrayal. Samson's enemies seized him, gouged out his eyes, clamped him in shackles and took him to Gaza where they imprisoned him (v. 21).

This is another instance in which we see a contrast between Samson and Christ. Jesus was tempted by Satan after fasting in the wilderness for forty days, but he was not careless. He challenged everything Satan said with God's Word, and if we follow his example we will not fall as Samson did.

There is a danger that, like Samson, we can toy with temptation, pushing the boundaries of what is acceptable as far as we can. Samson's experience shows us that the result will be disastrous. Rather than play games with Delilah, Samson should have read the warning signs and got out of the situation as quickly as possible. Many of us have memorized the famous verse that says: 'No temptation has seized you except what is common to man. And God is faithful; he will not let you be tempted beyond what you can bear. But when you are tempted, he will also provide a way out so that you can stand up under it' (1 Cor. 10:13). If we were to look at the context of this verse we would see that it tells us to be aware of spiritual danger that temptation places us in, and to escape the source of temptation as quickly as possible!

Had Samson thought about the consequences of yielding to sexual temptation he would have been spared the shame he had to endure. And the name of the Lord would not have been slandered by the Philistines who declared that their god, Dagon, had delivered Samson into their hands (vv. 23-24). If you are considering engaging in some form of sexual immorality, stop and consider where it will end. Speaking at a conference for church leaders, American pastor Rick Holland said: 'The consequences of immorality are inevitable and unavoidable. ... When it comes to sexual sin, it is payday someday! People talk, husbands find out, reporters snoop, pregnancies happen, diseases spread, guilt intensifies.'[19] This is something Samson discovered to his cost, and must be avoided by us at all costs!

Bringing the house down (vv. 22-31)

Samson's captors did not notice that his hair had begun to grow. This does not mean that his strength lay in his hair—it was from the Lord—but it did enable him to rededicate himself to his vows. The Puritan commentator Matthew Henry says that: 'The growth of his hair was neither the cause nor the sign of the return of his strength further than as it was the badge of his consecration, and a token that God accepted him as a Nazirite again, after the interruption, without those ceremonies which were appointed for the restoration of a lapsed Nazirite, which he had not now the opportunity of performing.'[20]

It was show-time! The Philistines had gathered in their temple for a big celebration; they offered sacrifices to their god, Dagon, and praised him for giving Samson into their hands. They then decided to bring him out to provide some entertainment, but this proved to be a massive miscalculation. He asked the young boy who led him to let him put his hands on the pillars and with the sound of 3,000 Philistines jeering in his ears he called out to the Lord: 'O Sovereign LORD, remember me. O God, please strengthen me just once more, and let me with one blow get revenge on the Philistines for my two eyes' (v. 28). Then he stood between the pillars and 'pushed with all his might, and down came the temple on the rulers and all the people in it' (v. 30). Samson killed more Philistines in that final act than throughout his entire life. Perhaps it was this act of sacrifice which gave him a place in the hall of the faithful recorded in Hebrews 11.

Samson was a child of his times. He lived in a day when 'everyone did as he saw fit' (21:25); one writer describes him as 'a sort of Israel in concentrated form.'[20] Although his life serves as a warning, his death is an assurance that it is never too late to call upon the Lord. However, when we do so our chief concern should be for God's glory rather than our own well-being.

Samson, the last of the judges, was very different from Gideon, Barak or Othniel. He had been given a monumental gift for a momentous mission, which he squandered. His life serves as a warning but his death gives hope of restoration to everyone who has fallen.

1. How would the warnings and practical advice set out in Proverbs 5 have helped Samson to avoid temptation? List the principles that should guide us in the way that we relate to members of the opposite sex (see also 1 Tim. 2:9-10; 5:2b).

2. What does James 1:13-15 tell us about the source and character of temptation? How must we resist it (see 1 Cor. 10:13; Prov. 6:27; Rom. 6:12-14)?

TO THINK ABOUT AND DISCUSS

1. Look at James 5:19-20 and consider how you would speak to a Christian friend who appears to be playing with the temptation to commit a sin such as adultery, fornication or theft. What should you do if he or she will not listen to you (see Matt. 18:15-19)?

2. A Christian leader has yielded to temptation and committed adultery. He leaves his position, repents of his sin and restores his relationship with his wife. Do you think that there should ever be a time when he might be allowed back into leadership or Christian ministry? If not, what should he be permitted to do?

3. What positive steps can local churches take to help men and women protect the purity of their marriage relationships?

13 Dangerous assumptions

(17:1-13)

I could be described as a 'Trekkie', that is, a fan of the science-fiction programme *Star Trek*. When I was a boy I avidly watched the classic episodes with Captain Kirk and Mr Spock. In my twenties and thirties I saw every *Star Trek* film released—at least twice—and watched the spin-off TV programmes such as *The Next Generation, Voyager* and *Deep Space Nine*.

The most recent *Star Trek* series, which is on TV at the time of writing this book, is called *Enterprise*, but it is very different from the other programmes because it is a prequel: the events happen in a time before the original series was set. This is so that avid 'Trekkies' can understand the events that led to the five-year mission undertaken by Captain Kirk and his crew in the first series. The last part of Judges (chapters 17-21) is to the rest of the book what *Enterprise* was to *Star Trek*.

Having outlined the 'ever-decreasing circles' of sin,

judgement, repentance and rescue by God, the writer now describes events that happened at the very beginning of this troubled period in Israel's history. We can be certain about this because 18:30 tells us that the Levite who is the central character of the chapter was a grandson of Moses. This detail places the events described in these chapters before the ministry of Othniel, who was the first judge. The events in these chapters are described to help us reflect on the roller-coaster ride we have undertaken throughout the last sixteen chapters. They also characterize the attitude of this dark period: 'In those days Israel had no king; everyone did as he saw fit' (17:6). The mindset of the era in which the book of Judges is set can be summed up by the contemporary phrase 'if it feels right do it.' And in chapters 17-21 we are told about the dangerous assumptions to which this led.

Home-made religion (vv. 1-13)

Chapter 17 revolves around a man called Micah who lived in the hill country of Ephraim. There is a note of irony in his name which meant 'who is like God' or 'God is incomparable'. Micah lived with his mother, but he would have been an adult at this time because we are told that he had a son whom he appointed to be a priest at his home-made shrine (v. 5).

From the very outset we are made to realize that he was not a man to be trusted. In his opening words he owned up to the theft of some silver that belonged to his mother, but he only did so because she uttered a curse against the person who had stolen it (v. 2). This led his mother to switch from a curse to a blessing, which she followed up with a pious intention: 'I solemnly consecrate my silver to the LORD for my son to make a carved image and a cast idol' (v. 3). Although it sounds sincere, it actually exposed her inconsistency. One minute she invoked a pagan curse and the next she was pronouncing a spiritual blessing in the name of the Lord. And she wanted her money used to make a carved image and a cast idol which was forbidden by God (Exod. 20:4)! She assumed that she knew what God wanted without checking it up with his commands.

> We may not worship images but when things like our hobbies, homes, possessions or family become more important than God they are idols.

Micah asked the local silversmith to melt the silver down and make it into an idol. He made a shrine and appointed his son as its priest. But the appointment was short-lived because Micah invited a young Levite from Bethlehem to assume the role. The young man was passing through and Micah made him an offer: he could live in his house 'as [his] father and priest' in return for board, lodging and money (vv. 7-10). This was highly irregular: the Levites were a tribe set apart by God to serve him as priests; they were allotted cities to live in and were to be supported by the rest of the population. However, as far as the young priest was concerned it was an offer he could not refuse, even though the shrine was full of idols. So Micah seized on the Levite's acceptance as a sign that the Lord would bless him (v. 13).

The idol factory

Micah had set up a shrine devoted to an idol and had encouraged a priest to forsake his God-given role. Yet because he had a priest in his home he assumed that God would bless him. The book of Jeremiah tells us that 'the heart is deceitful above all things' (Jer. 17:9) and Hebrews warns us against 'sin's deceitfulness' (Heb. 3:13). There are times when, like Micah, we convince ourselves that we are doing the right thing when we are actually disobeying God. We may even make our disobedience sound commendable; for example, instead of gossiping we are 'sharing an item for prayer'.

We may not worship images but when things like our hobbies, homes, possessions or family become more important than God they are idols. I once heard a retired pastor speak about the change he has seen in church attendance over his years of ministry. In his early years parents with young children would take it in turns to come to the evening service, but today it is more common for them all to stay at home to 'spend time with the family'. He went on to say that, while it is very important to have strong Christian families, there is a danger that we can make them into an idol or use them as an excuse to stay at home rather than to meet with God's people for worship.

For further study ▶

FOR FURTHER STUDY

1. What does the Bible teach about idols (see Exod. 20:4; 23:13; Ps. 81:9; Isa. 42:17; 1 Cor. 10:7)?

2. Read Amos 5:18-24 and Isaiah 1:10-17 and list the criticisms God levels at his people's worship. What does he require instead? Look up Mark 7:1-15 and compare this to the attitude and practice of the Pharisees.

TO THINK ABOUT AND DISCUSS

1. In what ways is the church of the twenty-first century comparable to Micah's home-made shrine? How have we let modern-day idolatry creep into the life of the church and what steps can we take to eradicate it?

2. Micah had convinced himself that he had done the right thing even though he had disobeyed God. Are there times when you have been so determined to do something that you have claimed it to be God's will? Think about the way in which you could have tested that belief.

14 Violent developments

(18:1-31)

The curtain lifts on chapter 18 with the news that the tribe of Dan was looking for a place to settle. When the Israelites first conquered Canaan the Danites were commanded to occupy the region between Ephraim and Judah. They did not take complete control of the territory and the tribes either side of them were much stronger, so they decided to relocate. They sent out five scouts who travelled through the area where Micah lived and stayed at his house.

Location, location, location! (vv. 1-31)

When they spoke to the young Levite whom Micah had employed in his shrine, they noticed that his accent was different to that of the local people. They asked him what he was doing there and he told them that he had been hired as Micah's personal priest. Once they had discovered this they thought that he could provide them with guidance from God, so they asked him whether their journey would be successful (v. 5). The priest told them exactly what they wanted to hear: 'Go in peace,' he said. 'Your journey has the LORD's approval' (v. 6). His words may sound very pious but in reality they were shallow. If the scouts had really wanted to know God's will they would have asked a Levite or a seer from their own region, someone who would have known them and asked hard questions. This man did not even bother to pray; in effect he was saying, 'Off you go and God be with you'.

The Danite scouts left Micah, setting off north to continue their quest. Eventually they found a region which seemed ideal at the foot of what is now called the Golan Heights. It was spacious and fertile but there was one problem—people were already living there!

The scouts returned home, enthusing about this potential new home. Since the inhabitants were 'unsuspecting and secure' (v. 7) the Danites decided to attack them, perceiving their lack of defence as a sign that 'God [had] put [the land] into [their] hands' (v. 10); so 600 men left to conquer the territory. They visited Micah's house to enlist the young Levite and told him that it would be better for him to serve a whole tribe rather than just one man and urged him to leave without telling his patron. Having already put himself up for hire, the young priest had no reservation about giving his services to the highest bidder, and with the help of the Danites, he 'took the ephod, the other household gods and the carved image' and left with them (v. 20). When Micah discovered what had happened he went out to find them and once he had caught them up he protested that they 'took the gods [he] made, and [his] priest, and went away' (v. 24). But they had overwhelming numbers and he could do no more than object.

When the Danites arrived at Laish (the territory they wanted as their new home) they mercilessly attacked the people living there (v. 27). About forty years earlier Joshua led the Israelites to conquer Canaan but Laish was not part of the territory they were commanded to occupy. The inhabitants of Laish were peaceful and secure, not cruel and war-like as the Canaanites were. But the Danites assumed that God wanted them to launch an attack on them. They could not fight the tough enemies they faced in the south—such as the Philistines and Ammonites—but they had no problem massacring the peaceful people of Laish. The Levite had said that their journey had the Lord's approval, the land had everything they wanted and the people were easy to defeat. This led them to assume that it was the Lord's will, but the idolatry that followed (see vv. 29-31) proves that they had no intention to serve God.

> The Puritan Thomas Watson wrote, 'Providence should be the Christian's diary but never his Bible.' We must not use circumstances to gauge whether we are doing the right thing; it is very easy to interpret them in such a way as to convince ourselves that we are doing what God wants of us, when that may not be the case.

The Puritan Thomas Watson wrote, 'Providence should be the Christian's diary but never his Bible.'[21] We must not use circumstances to gauge whether we are doing the right thing; it is very easy to interpret them in such a way as to convince ourselves that we are doing what God wants of us, when that may not be the case.

The Levite was prepared to tell the Danites what they wanted to hear. There are many people like him today who speak in God's name but lead us away from his will as revealed in the Bible. So it is vital that we 'test everything' (1 Thes. 5:21).

FOR FURTHER STUDY

1. What practices characterize a false prophet (see 1 Kings 1-14; Jer. 23:33-40; Neh. 6:12-14)?
2. Read Jude 4, 1 John 4:1-6 and 1 Timothy 4:1-3 and identify the hallmarks of a false teacher.

TO THINK ABOUT AND DISCUSS

1. Describe some of the false teaching that circulates in the church today. How does it conflict with the Word of God?
2. Do you think Christians are discerning enough? How can we be discerning without being overly suspicious of everyone?

15 What lies beneath

(19:1-30)

The closing three chapters in Judges are some of the most chilling in the Bible. The gruesome events we read about—which probably happened soon after the Israelites had taken possession of the Promised Land—expose the extent of the decay. 'Everyone did what was right in his own eyes' (21:25, ESV).

J udges 19-20 is a two-act drama, with some shocking twists. The first act begins with a touching scene of domestic reconciliation which turns to a violent tragedy (ch. 19); and the second act (ch. 20-21) begins with a tribal assembly and concludes with a massacre that almost wiped out the tribe of Benjamin.

A happy ending? (vv. 1-10)

Like the young man hired by Micah and later by the Danites, the Levite we are introduced to in chapter 19 came from Bethlehem and appeared to have no financial support.

Neither did he seem to have any real direction in life; he was 'sojourning in the remote parts of the hill country of Ephraim' (v. 1, ESV). The Levite had been living with a concubine (a woman with whom he had a physical relationship, but to whom he was not married[22]). The concubine was unfaithful to him and went back to live with her father. After four months the Levite decided it was time to do something to restore their relationship and he made the journey to her father's house 'to persuade her to return' (v. 3). In the original language the word translated 'persuade' conveys a sense of tenderness and intimacy. She was happy to see him and took him into her father's house. Her father oozed conviviality and it took the Levite several attempts to pack up his donkey and take his concubine home; in fact he did not leave for five days, and then it was the evening. On the surface it seems to be a happy ending, but we must be prepared for a shock!

An unfriendly town (vv. 11-21)

The Levite was on the road, gushing with rekindled love and longing to get back home but, since he had left in the evening, he did not get very far before nightfall. The nearest town was a place called Jebus (which later became known as Jerusalem). When his servant suggested that they stop there for the night the Levite decided against it because it was 'an alien city, whose people [were] not Israelites' (v. 12) and planned instead to stop at Gibeah or Ramah, towns which would have been populated by their own people. (At this point the people of Israel had not driven out the inhabitants of Jebus and settled in it.)

On the surface the Levite seemed to have a good point. It would have been much better for him to be among his own people; in fact they should have been honoured to have a Levite among them. However, events do not unfold as we might expect. When they arrived at Gibeah 'they went and sat in the city square, but no one took them into his home for the night' (v. 14). That was unusual; if a Jew visited a town in his homeland he would wait at the central place and expect offers of hospitality. But in this instance none were forthcoming.

Eventually help arrived from an old man, who was a migrant himself. He told the Levite that he was welcome to stay the night at his home and that he would 'supply whatever [he needed]', giving some urgent advice: 'Only don't spend the night in the square' (20). This signalled that something was seriously wrong. If we were watching this scene in a film it would be accompanied by dramatic music suggesting that there is great danger looming.

Uninvited guests (vv. 22-30)

Initially, however, there seemed to be little sign of trouble; the Levite, his concubine and servant went to the man's home, ate a meal, and prepared to rest. The relaxed atmosphere was suddenly broken by a knock at the door and the sinister reality of this inhospitable town began to surface. 'While they were enjoying themselves, some of the wicked men of the city surrounded the house. Pounding on the door, they shouted to the old man who owned the house, "Bring out the man who came to your house so we can have sex with him"' (v. 22).

The scene is similar to one we read about in Genesis, when Lot entertained the two angels who visited him during the time he lived in Sodom. Wicked men encircled Lot's house saying, 'Where are the men who came to you tonight? Bring them out to us so that we can have sex with them' (see Gen. 19:4-5). But the shocking difference between the two events is that Sodom was a pagan city which came under God's judgement, while this was a town inhabited by God's people in the land he had provided for them.

In order to protect his guest, the host made the mob a distasteful offer: 'Look, here is my virgin daughter, and his concubine. I will bring them out to you now, and you can use them and do to them whatever you wish. But to this man, don't do such a disgraceful thing' (v. 24). Earlier in the narrative the Levite 'spoke tenderly' to his concubine in order to win her back. So now we would have expected him bravely to defend her honour, but the writer hits us with another shock-wave. After they refused to listen, the Levite 'took his concubine and sent her outside to them' (v. 25). The Hebrew word means that he shoved her out. The result was appalling: after inflicting a night of rape and sexual abuse upon her, the vile mob left her to stagger back to the door of the house where she lay until daybreak. When the Levite opened the door he was not 'speaking tenderly' to her as he had done before; instead he ordered her to get up because they were leaving. She was either dead or unconscious, so he 'put her on his donkey and set out for home' (v. 28). When he arrived he did something atrocious: 'he took a knife and cut up his concubine, limb by limb, into twelve parts and sent them into all the areas of Israel (v. 29).

This is a particularly shocking account. The Israelites were acting like people from Sodom and the Levite treated the woman whom he had gone to such lengths to win back with appalling cruelty. Instead of giving her the dignity of a burial he sliced her up and spread her remains around the country. We may wonder why such a hideous event is recorded in the Bible; but it does show us that in spite of being God's people, the Israelites of this era were no different from the people who lived in Sodom or Canaan.

It is easy to read a distressing story like this and conclude that we could not possibly be as cruel and wicked as the characters it describes, but if we do so we will not be challenged by the message. The incident recounted in this chapter urges us to ask a searching question: What lies beneath our claim to be God's people? We may take the name of Christian, meet with God's people, and say all the right things; but the reality beneath the surface could be very different. J.B. Phillips wrote a skilful paraphrase of Romans 12:2 saying, 'Do not let the world squeeze you into its own mould.'23 Rather than following the dictates of our culture and doing 'what is right in [our] own eyes' we must be sure to live under the rule of our King, the Lord Jesus, and obey his Word.

FOR FURTHER STUDY

1. What were the similarities between the behaviour of the people of Israel and that of the citizens of Sodom and Gomorrah (see Gen. 19:1-11)?

How does their behaviour conflict with the commands set out in Leviticus 18:22 and 20:13?

2. In what ways are these practices a sign of God's judgement (see Rom. 1:24-32)?

TO THINK ABOUT AND DISCUSS

1. How much time should the church invest in campaigning about moral issues such as abortion and pornography?

2. What can we do to reach people caught up in the practices we read about in Romans 1?

16 Chain reaction

(20:1-21:25)

The Levite's macabre act got people's attention and the general consensus was that nothing like this had happened since they left Egypt, and that something had to be done (19:30).

These events happened shortly after Joshua had taken them into the Promised Land so there was still a strong sense of unity among the tribes of Israel. This enabled them to organize a huge assembly of 'Israelites from Dan to Beersheba' (the territory that lay the furthest north and south). The gathering took place at Mizpah, which was on the border of the territory of the tribe of Benjamin and therefore near to where these terrible events had taken place. It would have been a huge gathering, with the tribal leaders meeting at the central location and the mass of people setting up camp in the surrounding area. Their meeting appeared to have a spiritual tone; the writer tells us that it was 'before the Lord', but—as we will discover—this was another façade.

A corrupted case (20:4-48)

As the guest of honour, the Levite was invited to speak, and he put his case very eloquently. He was dramatic (v. 5a), and he played on their emotions (v. 5b), saying that he had made his macabre response 'because they committed this lewd and disgraceful act in Israel' (v. 6). And he concluded by challenging them to act: 'Now, all you Israelites, speak up and give your verdict' (v. 7). It was a skilful display of oratory which brought about the response that he would have wanted. But he had twisted the truth. He said the men intended to kill him, when they were actually looking for sex. He did not tell them that his concubine died because he pushed her out of the door to protect himself. He failed to given them details of the callous way he acted the next morning when he found his concubine laying on the doorstep. He made sure that he looked as virtuous as possible!

Tragic unity

The Levite's skilful speech provoked a response from the other tribes. They were united in their grief about these terrible events and 'wept before the LORD until evening' (v. 23). It may appear as if something positive had emerged from this atrocity but we should not miss the tragic irony. Although they were focused on God, united in their grief and prayerful about their response, they joined together against the tribe of Benjamin rather than against the Ammonites or Canaanites. In fact the writer emphasizes this by reminding us that the Benjamites were 'their fellow Israelites' (v. 13) and their 'brothers' (vv. 23,28). Despite this they were treated no differently from the Canaanites at the time when Joshua first led the people of Israel to possess the Promised Land (see vv. 37,48).

In denial

The tribe of Benjamin had been conspicuous by their absence, but the remaining tribes wanted to give them the opportunity to hand over the perpetrators of this crime so that they might be brought to justice. However, they refused (v. 12). The reason behind this may be related to the confidence they placed in their army of 700 left-handed soldiers, described by Dale Ralph Davis as 'an elite corps of left-handed super-slingers'.[24] This would have made them quite formidable, because most soldiers were right-handed and would have held their shield in their left hand (which would not have defended them against these left-handed slingers); but the Benjamites' confidence was misplaced and the result was devastating:

On that day twenty-five thousand Benjamite swordsmen fell, all of them valiant fighters. But six hundred men turned and fled into the desert to the rock of Rimmon, where they stayed for four months. The men of Israel went back to Benjamin and put all the towns to the sword, including the animals and everything else they found. All the towns they came across they set on fire (vv. 46-48). If they had faced up to the evil that lay within their borders the outcome would have been very different.

Although reading the 'religious news' in the press can be a depressing exercise, if we are not careful it can also make us feel very smug. There are some terrible ideas and practices among people who call themselves Christians but there are also many things needing to be put right in churches that are faithful to the Bible. We must also look very carefully at our own lives, asking God to show us where we are at variance with his Word.

Misguided correctives (21:1-24)

The smoke was pouring out from the tribe of Benjamin's territory, the dust of the battle was beginning to settle and the reality of the whole brutal episode had begun to dawn on the remaining eleven tribes. One of their tribes was almost annihilated and in the heat of the moment they had vowed that none of their daughters would be allowed to marry a Benjamite. This presented them with a problem: 'How can we provide wives for those who are left?' (v. 7). If they were to do nothing the tribe of Benjamin would die out.

> Although reading the 'religious news' in the press can be a depressing exercise, if we are not careful it can also make us feel very smug.

They had also vowed that anyone who had not joined the assembly would be put to death. When they discovered that no one from Jabesh Gilead had been present they decided to use the second vow to get them out of the mess the first one had got them into. They killed everyone in Jabesh Gilead except the young virgins who would provide wives for the 600 surviving Benjamite men. There was a dark logic at work which reflected the way in which 'everyone did as he saw fit'. They kept the vow not to allow any other women to marry a Benjamite but they considered it appropriate to give them the survivors of a massacre they had instigated, as wives.

There was still a shortfall of women, so they turned to kidnapping. Soldiers from Benjamin were sent to a festival at a village called Shiloh where the young women would have danced, giving the soldiers an ideal opportunity to grab a wife for themselves.

These two solutions—one cruel and the other almost comical—betrayed the attitude that prevailed in this sad chapter in Israel's history: 'In those days there was no king in Israel. Everyone did what was right in his own eyes' (v. 25, ESV). The writer is reflecting from the standpoint of a time when there was a king ruling Israel. There were some great kings who led the people to love and serve God; there were also many spectacular failures. But now the King of kings has come. He has dealt with the root of the problem—sin—and will return to judge this world (see Acts 10:42). Let us live in the light of the kingdom that he has established.

FOR FURTHER STUDY

1. Read Judges 1:8,17 and compare the treatment of the tribe of Benjamin with their attack on the Canaanites.

2. The book closes by telling us that 'in those days Israel had no king; everyone did as he saw fit' (Judg. 21:25). Can we conclude, from this comment, that a king would address their problems (see 1 Sam. 8)?

TO THINK ABOUT AND DISCUSS

1. When is it right to divide from people who call themselves Christians? Think about this in relation to some of the major doctrinal issues that are under discussion today.

2. Are we in danger of setting our hopes on men rather than on the Lord? How do we get the balance between seeking strong biblical leadership and individually doing God's will while depending on his power?

Further reading

Arthur Cundall, *Judges and Ruth*, Tyndale Old Testament Commentaries, IVP

Dale Ralph Davis, *Judges*, Christian Focus Publications

Alfred Edersheim, *The Bible History—Old Testament*, Eerdmans

C.J. Goslinga, *Joshua, Judges, Ruth—Bible Student's Commentary*, Zondervan

Leon Wood, The *Distressing Days of the Judges*, Wipf and Stock Publishers

Keddie, Gordon J, *Even in Darkness*, Evangelical Press, Welwyn, 1985

Endnotes

1 I am grateful to my friend Chris Hughes for suggesting this description.

2 See Davis, Dale Ralph, *Judges*, Christian Focus Publications, 2003, p. 49.

3 Edersheim, Alfred, *The Bible History— Old Testament*, Eerdmans, 1992, p. 119.

4 Grudem, Wayne, *Systematic Theology*, Zondervan, 1994, p. 515.

5 Myers, M., quoted by Cundall, Arthur, *Judges and Ruth*, Tyndale Old Testament Commentaries, IVP, 1968, p. 108.

6 This can be calculated from the figures given in 7:3.

7 Spurgeon, C.H., *Treasury of the Bible*, Waterlow and Songs, 1962, p. 554.

8 Wood, Leon, *The Distressing Days of the Judges*, Wipf and Stock Publishers, 1998, p. 243.

9 Davis, *Judges*, p. 146.

10 See Henry, M., *Matthew Henry's Commentary on the Whole Bible: Complete and unabridged in one volume*, Hendrickson, electronic version; Keddie, Gordon, *Even in darkness*, Welwyn Commentary Series, Evangelical Press, 1985; Wood, *Distressing Days of the Judges*, pp. 287-295.

11 See Davis, *Judges*, pp. 146-149.

12 Goslinga, C.J., *Joshua, Judges, Ruth—Bible Student's Commentary*, Zondervan, 1987, p. 395.

13 See Joshua 13:3 and 1 Samuel 14:1-47.

14 See 2 Samuel 5:17-25.

15 See Cundall, *Judges and Ruth*, p. 163.

16 As above.

17 Moffat translation, quoted in Davis, *Judges*, p. 184.

18 Wood, *Distressing Days of the Judges*, p. 379.

19 Holland, Rick, spoken at the *Shepherds' Conference*, Grace Community Church, Sun Valley, Los Angeles, 2002.

1 Henry, *Commentary on the Whole Bible*.

20 Davis, *Judges*, p. 192.

21 Watson, Thomas, *A Body of Divinity*, Banner of Truth, 1983, p. 123.

22 'The difference between wife and concubine was less marked among the Hebrews than among us, owing

to the absence of moral stigma. The difference probably lay in the absence of the right of the bill of divorce, without which the wife could not be repudiated' (*Smith's Bible Dictionary*, <http://bible.crosswalk.com/Diction aries/SmithsBibleDictionary/>)

23 Phillips, J.B, *Translation of the New Testament*, <http://www.ccel.org/bible/phillips/ CP06Romans2.htm>
24 Davis, *Judges*, p. 218.

OPENING UP JUDGES

OPENING UP JUDGES

OPENING UP JUDGES

ALSO FROM SIMON J ROBINSON

FACE2FACE WITH ELIJAH

ENCOUNTERING GOD'S FIERY PROPHET

SIMON J ROBINSON

Elijah lived in a time of intense spiritual darkness. People were openly disobeying God's commands, and true worship seemed to have been all but snuffed out. And yet God was still at work! Bringing the power of his word and Spirit into this situation, he used Elijah to break the darkness and to draw people back to himself.

PAPERBACK, 80PP, £4, ISBN 978 1 84625 011 8,

OPENING UP 1 TIMOTHY

SIMON J ROBINSON

1 Timothy is an urgent letter to a Christian in the thick of a crisis and a call to the local church to get on with the job God has called

it to do—spreading the good news! Simon Robinson applies this message incisively to modern readers.

This is not only a commentary of very practical insights but also of cogent exegetical conclusions. The author's no-nonsense approach is particularly helpful in getting to the heart of the text, while maintaining strong pastoral exhortations. It will be a well-worn tool both for the preacher and the diligent believer. Jerry Wragg, Pastor-Teacher, Grace Immanuel Bible Church, Jupiter, Florida

128PP PAPERBACK, £5, ISBN 978 1 903087 69 4,

GOD, THE BIBLE AND TERRORISM

SIMON J ROBINSON

A graphically yet sensitively illustrated booklet, considering points such as 'How would Jesus respond to the London bombings?', 'Is this God's judgement?', 'Forgiveness and justice' and 'Seeking the Lord while he may still be found'.

16PP BOOKLET, ILLUSTRATED COLOUR THROUGHOUT, £0.50P, ISBN 978 1 84625 017 X

'Simon challenges us to ... look at our own lives and how we will respond to the Judge of all the Earth when our time inevitably comes to meet him.' MARK MULLINS

DISCOUNTS FOR QUANTITY PURCHASES

The
Opening
up
series

Opening up
Exodus

Opening up
Ezra

Opening up
Psalms

Opening up
Ecclesiastes

Opening up
Ezekiel's visions

Opening up
Amos

Opening up
Nahum

Opening up
1 Corinthians

Further
titles in
preparation

Opening up
Philippians

Opening up
1 Thessalonians

Opening up
1 Timothy

Opening up
2 & 3 John

This fine series is aimed at the 'average person in the church' and combines brevity, accuracy and readability with an attractive page layout. Thought-provoking questions make the books ideal for both personal or small group use.

'Laden with insightful quotes and penetrating practical application, Opening up Philippians is a Bible study tool which belongs on every Christian's bookshelf!'

DR. PHIL ROBERTS, PRESIDENT, MIDWESTERN BAPTIST THEOLOGICAL SEMINARY, KANSAS CITY, M I S S O U R I

Please contact us for a free catalogue

In the UK ☎ 01568 613 740   **email—** sales@dayone.co.uk

In the United States: ☎ Toll Free: 1-8-morebooks

In Canada: ☎ 519 763 0339 www.dayone.co.uk